T0114276

THE POLITICAL THOUGHT OF LUIS MUÑOZ MARÍN

14410-RIVE

THE POLITICAL THOUGHT OF LUIS MUÑOZ MARÍN

José A. Rivera

14410-RIVE

Copyright © 2002 by José A. Rivera.

ISBN: Softcover   1-4010-4672-X

All rights reserved. No part of this book may be reproduced or transmitted in any form or by any means, electronic or mechanical, including photocopying, recording, or by any information storage and retrieval system, without permission in writing from the copyright owner.

This book was printed in the United States of America.

To order additional copies of this book, contact:
Xlibris Corporation
1-888-795-4274
www.Xlibris.com
Orders@Xlibris.com

CONTENTS

To José Antonio, Fe, and Juanín

14410-RIVE

Freedom takes many forms, and the form should be suited to the society, not the society to the form.

Luis Muñoz Marín

ACKNOWLEDGEMENTS

I would like to express my gratitude to the following persons for their contribution to this project: Iván Calderón and the staff of the *Centro de Cómputos Académico* of the *Universidad del Sagrado Corazón*, Giannina Delgado Caro, Julio E. Quirós Alcalá, and José Ramón González from the *Fundación Luis Muñoz Marín*, George McLean and Robert Sokolowski from The Catholic University of America, Marshall Morris from the University of Puerto Rico, Antonio J. Colorado, and Elsa Tió.

PROLOGUE

This work by José Rivera is the most serious effort to date to comprehend, analytically and philosophically, the political thought of Luis Muñoz Marín. As such, it clarifies the philosophical foundations on which the institutional structure of contemporary Puerto Rican society has been erected.

The work of Muñoz has been fundamental in the political, economic and social spheres. The values that shaped our particular democracy, our political relationship with the United States, our economy and the restructuring of our society have their beginning point in his thinking.

The task of putting Muñoz's ideas, which are dispersed throughout his literary, political and governmental writings, into an orderly formulation has been both difficult and necessary. The evaluation that Rivera makes within what he calls perennial philosophy is an important contribution to understanding the universality of the thinking of this Puerto Rican who most closely approached the Platonic ideal of the ruler par excellence.

The book comes to us at an appropriate moment. These are fateful times for democracy in Puerto Rico and for our political status. Fateful for democracy, for profound reasons that go beyond the behavior of those who govern us, behavior that places strains on the republican form of our system of government and keeps public opinion in a state of high tension. The deepest reasons have to do with the concentration of economic power, the exercise of political power which is not responsive to the will of the people, the dramatic changes which have come about as a result of the growth of the communications media, the capacity for manipulation by these powers, the breakdown of the ethical principles which guide the behavior of individuals, and the absence of cohesive values reflecting the collective aspirations of society.

The power of the vote is not nearly as great today as it was in Muñoz's time. The operation of the electoral mandate is mediatized today by very powerful forces. This is a problem not only for Puerto Rico but throughout the world. The United States is greatly affected by this, but conventional wisdom holds the leaders who happen to be in power responsible, without realizing that they are not the source of the problem.

The importance of the political thinking of Muñoz on the contemporary problems of democracy and the issue of political status is not to be found in the particular institutional form that was given these ideas some 50 years ago. These forms have clearly been overwhelmed by circumstance and need reformulation in keeping with present needs. But the values that inspired those actions in the past remain as valid as ever: human dignity, full development of individual potential, social justice, the value of the cultures of the different peoples, the wholeness of freedom, and both personal and collective autonomy achieved in the virtuous exercise of freedom.

The possibility of governing contemporary Puerto Rico in such a way as to move our society toward what Muñoz called a great civilization is beyond the capacity of the democratic and governmental instruments available to us today. In this sense, to forge a common purpose is a difficult task. But it is an indispensable task that must be accomplished on the basis of the values that inspired Muñoz and the experience of these 50 years which calls for the reformulation of the institutions which Muñoz's thought bequeathed to contemporary Puerto Rico.

The United States is experiencing its own difficulties of governance, and it is acting with systematic negligence in regard to its responsibility concerning the status of Puerto Rico. US politics has a long way to go to overcome the predominantly superficial, short-term style that has characterized it and so to rise to the level of its historic responsibility toward Puerto Rico. The year 1998 will mark 100 years of this shameful history of moral evasion.

That is why I think it very appropriate that José Rivera's volume on the political thought of Muñoz Marín, with its profound moral content, should appear at this time, and I appreciate the honor of being asked to provide this prologue.

Rafael Hernández Colón
Governor of Puerto Rico
1973-76, 1985-92

INTRODUCTION

Luis Muñoz Marín (1898-1980)—poet, story-teller, journalist, orator, and statesman—led the peaceful revolution which transformed Puerto Rico from a poor, agrarian economy to a modern, industrial one, from an island beggared by adversity, to one of the most progressive countries in the world. He is also the creator of a new form of political association with the United States—the *Estado Libre Asociado* or Commonwealth of Puerto Rico—based on equal dignity, one that enriches not only American constitutional thought but also the principles of federalism and democracy in general. Muñoz was decorated in many countries, including Panama, France and Peru. He was given honorary degrees by universities such as Harvard, Brandeis, Middlebury and Rutgers, and was honored by The Freedom House and other international organizations. President Lyndon B. Johnson, upon granting him the Medal of Liberty, the highest civil award in the United States, summarized Muñoz's life as follows: "A poet, politician, public servant, and patriot. He has led his people to new heights of dignity and purpose, and has transformed a stricken land into a vital society."[1] Though Muñoz enjoys worldwide recognition as a political genius, no attempt has been made to expound his thought in a systematic fashion, and to uncover its philosophical presuppositions and relate it to traditional values by articulating it in terms of the perennial philosophy. This book, based on a doctoral dissertation presented at The Catholic University of America in Washington, D.C., represents a contribution toward that goal.[2]

Muñoz, an autodidact and eclectic deeply influenced by Fabianism, had an ample and positive conception of freedom.

He knew that the given end of man is what philosophers refer to as the Good Life, and that politics is concerned with choosing the right means to this end. The political status of a people, for example, is a means to an end or, at most, an interim goal, but one can become obsessed with a status option (e.g., statehood or independence) if one views it as the end itself; one can be the servant rather than the master of such a goal. Muñoz thus criticized the utopianism of those who place their ideologies above the common good and treat the people as a juridical entity instead of as a human community. He concluded that a political status that obstructed the shaping of a great civilization would not give real freedom to the people of Puerto Rico.

Considering that human nature tends toward, and is fulfilled by, participation in a greater whole, Muñoz believed that larger associations of peoples enjoy greater freedom than do smaller groups isolated from one another as independent nations. Muñoz never saw the relationship between the United States and Puerto Rico as based exclusively on economic deficiencies of the island; he thought it rested on a genuine friendship brought about by history and shared values regarding religion, justice, and democracy. This type of communion is the core of political life.

As a distinct culture and nationality, Puerto Rico should, Muñoz thought, preserve its unique identity, embodying enduring values such as language, while yet taking part in the common good of the United States. He believed that the Commonwealth should cultivate the greatest degree of autonomy compatible with American citizenship. Muñoz says: "All that restricts the authority of Puerto Rico in Puerto Rico without any appreciable advantage to the Union, and without being essential to the principle of association through common citizenship, should be removed from the compact in some proper manner at some proper time."[3] Convinced that freedom and cooperation are complementary, Muñoz claimed that the development of the Commonwealth concept, far from implying separation, means a deeper and stronger union.

The works of Luis Muñoz Marín can be found in the *Archivo Luis Muñoz Marín* at the *Fundación Luis Muñoz Marín* in Río Piedras, Puerto Rico. Though my research addressed all the pertinent sections of the *Archivo*, I concentrated on the material found in Section V, which refers to Muñoz's governorship of Puerto Rico from 1949 to 1964.[4] It is here that one finds the mature thought of Muñoz articulating solutions to the economic, social and political problems of Puerto Rico. The years covered by this section witness Muñoz's creation and defense of the Commonwealth status as the answer to the island's political predicament. Undoubtedly, the bulk of Muñoz's intellectual work appears in the form of speeches. He employed his official and political speeches as the vehicle for a unique rhetoric that reaches the wealthy and the poor, the educated and the illiterate alike, teaching, persuading, and leading them towards the realization of their ideals. Of course the speeches as such are only a part of the immense legacy of human betterment Muñoz left behind.

NOTES

1. Ana M. Ortiz Salichs and María Hernández Rodríguez, eds., *Luis Muñoz Marín: bibliografía mínima* (Ponce: Centro de Estudios Puertorriqueños, 1991), iii.

2. José A. Rivera, "Political Autonomy and the Good in the Thought of Yves R. Simon and Luis Muñoz Marín" (Ph.D. diss., The Catholic University of America, 1993).

3. Luis Muñoz Marín, Address delivered at the University of Kansas City on 23 April 1955, *Archivo Luis Muñoz Marín*, *Fundación Luis Muñoz Marín*, Río Piedras, Puerto Rico. Except when otherwise indicated, all references to Muñoz's works relate to the *Archivo Luis Muñoz Marín* at the *Fundación Luis Muñoz Marín* in Río Piedras, Puerto Rico.

4. The *Archivo* consists of 15 Sections organized under the following headings: (I) Personal File; (II) First Years, 1898-1936; (III) The Politician, 1920-1940; (IV) President of the Senate, 1941-1948; (V) Governor of Puerto Rico, 1949-1964; (VI) Senator, 1965-1970; (VII) The Statesman, 1970-1980; (VIII) Diplomas, Plaques, Certificates of Honor; (IX) Printed Materials, and Newspapers; (X) Audio-Visual Material; (XI) Obituaries, Posthumous Expressions and Acknowledgements; (XIII) Private Collections of Collaborators of Luis Muñoz Marín; (XIV) Oral History; and (XV) Personal File of Doña Inés María Mendoza de Muñoz Marín. Each of these sections is divided into series and sub-series, some of which are further divided into yet smaller

categories. All this documentation is kept in boxes and folders. To find a document in the *Archivo*, however, a researcher need only give its title (if any), description, and date, since the archivists are then able to locate it physically.

The central part of the *Archivo* contains a vast collection of documents related to Muñoz's literary, journalistic, and political careers, covering the years from 1917 to 1940, his endeavors as founder of the Popular Democratic Party and president of the Senate from 1941 to 1948, as governor of Puerto Rico from 1949 to 1964, as senator from 1965 to 1970, and as statesman from 1970 to 1980. Among the literary works to be found in the *Archivo* are poems in Spanish such as "Salmo del dios andrajoso," "Cantos de la Humanidad Forcejeando," "Primavera," "La Canción de los Bostezos," and poems in English such as "Moods," "Queries," and "Leaves." He translated his own poems and of poets such as José Santos Chocano, Edgar Lee Masters, Carl Sandburg and Edwin Markham, some of whom he met, as well as wrote essays in literary criticism such as "Poetas de la democracia" and "Song Maker of a Continent." His work in prose consists of short stories, *Borrones* (1917), and a collection of novels, *Madre Haraposa* (1918). Other books by Muñoz are his two-volume autobiography, *Memorias* (1982, 1992), and *La historia del Partido Popular Democrático* (1984).

As a journalist, in his youth, Muñoz published numerous articles, essays and editorials, both in Spanish and English, in newspapers and magazines of Puerto Rico—*La Democracia*, *El Mundo*, *Puerto Rico Ilustrado*, *La Linterna*, *Juan Bobo*—and of the United States—*World's Work*, *The Baltimore Sun*, *The American Mercury*, *The Nation*, *The New Republic*—covering a wide variety of local, American, Hispanic-American and European themes. He addressed local political, social, and economic problems, government and party politics, and issues of Puerto Rican culture. During 1922-1923 he published a series of articles in *La Democracia* which dealt with criticism of United States literature, drama, politics, and lifestyles.

The *Archivo* contains a huge collection of private and public documents from Muñoz's political life. These include letters to officials of local, federal, or foreign governments; ecclesiastical authorities; Puerto Rican, American, and Latin American intellectuals; foreign diplomats and dignitaries; international celebrities; and professional, civic, cultural, labor and scientific associations at home and abroad. There are also public documents of diverse origin and nature such as executive orders, laws, acts, rulings, legislative resolutions, policies, agreements, budgets, state of the Commonwealth addresses, speeches, statements, messages, records of official acts, official publications, press conferences, press releases, memos, cables, telegrams, maps, graphs, diagrams, etc. Also included are talks, lectures, newspaper articles, interviews, and audio-visual material such as photographs, films, records and tapes. In 1959, Muñoz was invited by Harvard University to give the annual lecture series known as the Godkin Lectures. His drafts for this occasion on the topic, "Breakthrough from Nationalism: A Small Island Looks at Big Trouble," are also kept in the *Archivo*. All these materials constitute a primary source of information for studies about a wide variety of subjects: the political, economic, social and cultural thought of Muñoz, the issue of the political status of Puerto Rico, the nature, origin and development of the Commonwealth, public administration, public health, social and labor legislation, Muñoz's American and international roles, and his defense of democracy and religion. Muñoz's state of the Commonwealth addresses have been published in a book entitled *Mensajes al pueblo puertorriqueño* (1980), and his official speeches from 1949 to 1952 have been collected into a volume called *Discursos oficiales* (1973). The *Fundación Luis Muñoz Marín* plans to publish the complete works of Muñoz by the year 1998 in celebration of the 100th anniversary of his birth.

CHAPTER 1

MUÑOZ'S IDEAL OF THE GOOD FOR PUERTO RICO

"Man does not live by bread alone," wrote Luis Muñoz Marín, "[but] by his love of God, which is love of the good."[5] For Muñoz, man, more than a mere *individual,* is a *person* of infinite worth, whether he be European or Chinese, a doctor or a shoeshine boy.[6] Individuals differ in nationality, occupation, wealth, and social standing but all have equal value as persons. Similarly, societies differ in geographical size, wealth, and might but all have equal dignity before God. Muñoz recognized that individual men and human communities have a spiritual dimension which accounts for tendencies and needs beyond material concerns. Hence the satisfaction of the material needs of man—though for Muñoz an essential and noble ideal—cannot be for him the final purpose in life. The final goal of man is what he called "la vida buena"[7] (literally, the good life, a life which is good):

> good occupations, understanding, good neighbor-
> liness, art and study, serenely making sure that
> there is good government, and deepening, so far
> as God grants us the light to do so, reverent friend-
> ship with Him.[8]

This "cultural ideal"[9] —as Muñoz also called it—obviously

implies the full development of our humanness. Since our humanness does not arise in an empty vacuum but emerges only
within the matrix of being Puerto Ricans (it is in Puerto Rico
that we have become men and women), the shaping of our humanness is intimately related to the shaping of our identity as
Puerto Ricans and the latter depends on the former:

> We know that Puerto Rican culture . . . is and will
> be part of the great culture of the West. But there
> is no such thing as a Westerner who is not from
> some particular place in the West. If we are not
> Westerners with Puerto Rican roots, we are root-
> less Westeners. . . . We are a Western people in
> the way our roots have shaped us.[10]

Part of the good life as defined by Muñoz is also man's aware-
ness of his relation to the universe, that is, his religious conscious-
ness, "the sense man has of being part of a vast universal purpose
which is the will of God."[11] Man, who possesses a creative free
will given to him by the divine plan, is always looking for ways
to make his life "agreeable to that universal purpose—which is
the good."[12]

Naturally the good for man has several aspects, and these
correspond to the various dimensions of his complex being. These
diverse aspects of the good Muñoz labeled "ideals."[13] He distinguished between economic, political, and cultural ideals (which
he also called economic, political, and cultural "freedoms") as
essential components of the good for a human community.[14]
One cannot build a culture upon human misery, for example, so
the cultural ideal presupposes an "economic ideal"[15] as a necessary though not sufficient condition of the good life. Muñoz
concretely defined the economic ideal for Puerto Rico as follows:

> A minimum of Goods for each family, . . . includ-

> ing good shelter, adequate nutrition, clothing,
> education, recreation, the opportunity of acquir-
> ing some skill . . . and of serving disinterestedly,
> and security for times of misfortune and old age."[16]

According to Muñoz, the attainment of this "economic freedom"[17] or "social justice"[18] depends on abundance of production
and a fair distribution of that abundance.

In order to preserve and cultivate in the people the spiritual
values of the cultural ideal and to ensure its material conditions,
in other words, to guide the collective action of the people towards the good life, a government or authority is needed to harmonize the many individual wills into a unified whole. Muñoz
conceived of the "political ideal" for Puerto Rico in terms of a
"democratic life within a republican form of government."[19] In
his view, this ideal has two aspects: (a) the genuine practice of
democracy and (b) the adoption of a morally and juridically valid
political status. Muñoz observed that democracy "considers the
personality of the individual as something sacred."[20] He interpreted democracy philosophically as a specific attitude towards
life and death that fuses with the religious spirit, in particular,
with Christianity:

> In its deepest sense, democracy must be defined
> as an attitude of deep equality among human be-
> ings, . . . equality of human dignity facing life and
> death, . . . equality of the human soul before hu-
> man life.[21]

Of course the democratic life implies self-determination and
self-government by the people, since democracy *is* government
of the people, by the people and for the people. Power through
the votes of Puerto Ricans on election day, to give them more
control over their own destiny—that was how Muñoz defined
the essence of democracy.[22] Democracy thus implies the aboli-

tion of all kinds of domination, servitude and despotism, which for Puerto Rico meant surpassing its colonial political status as war booty from the Spanish-American conflict of 1898.

According to Muñoz, not only democracy and political status, but their interrelationship as well, must also be included in the political ideal. In his inaugural address of 1953, he claimed, for example, that the practice of democracy demands that the right of the people be recognized to choose the government it wishes, and that a political status, whether traditional or new in form, freely approved and chosen by the majority of the people, should be respected and supported even by those who voted against it, who do not approve of it, or who criticize it. It is a matter of conscience, Muñoz thought, to be loyal to the decision of the majority for the sake of the health of the community. It is patriotic duty, he felt, that requires that no one denigrate the constitution:

> To interpret the Commonwealth meanspiritedly is clearly to fail in our duty towards Puerto Rico and is disloyal to the good name of the United States.[23]
>
> *   *   *
>
> It is everyone's duty, out of loyalty to Puerto Rico and the United States, to give the highest and most dignified interpretation to the political status that we have.[24]

While democracy allows for discrepancy and respects the rights of minorities, it also protects the right of the majority not to be forced into the views of the minority. Muñoz thus contended that no one had the authority to interpret the political status chosen by the people of Puerto Rico as being something less than what this people understands it to be:

Every constitution is subject to different interpretations which are made in good faith. But my thesis is that by their votes in the referenda in which Public Law 600 and the Constitution were approved, the people adopted the interpretations of these documents advanced by those who campaigned for their approval. We submit that when the time comes for judicial review of the compact and the Constitution, they should be interpreted in accordance with the understanding of the people as to their meaning and scope when they approved them.[25]

These three components of the common good—the economic ideal, the political ideal, and the cultural ideal—are inextricably bound together. They are inseparable, not only from the common good as such but also from each other. Muñoz pointed out, for example, that without economic freedom not only is there no common good, but the political and cultural freedoms are diminished. On the other hand, economic production without culture leads to consumerism, while a culture without social justice is self-contradictory. Similarly, self-government without social justice is a failure, while without political freedom both culture and social justice are lessened. The economic, political, and cultural ideals are inseparable, essential to the good life and to one another. The absence of any one of these unravels the good life as a whole, and so affects the other elements.

Hence Muñoz concluded that the realization of the good life by the people demands the realization of ALL these ideals—the economic, the political, and the cultural, and that the concrete freedom in which this good life is enjoyed requires ALL the freedoms—the economic, the political, and the cultural. This implies, for example, that economic freedom is not to be achieved at the expense of political freedom, nor political freedom at the expense of economic freedom. Muñoz thus sought economic solvency for Puerto Rico—not, however, in terms of the tyranny he saw, for example, in Cuba—but in terms of liberty, democracy, and respect for human beings. This conviction that the distinct human freedoms should not be at odds with one another but should, on the contrary, work together towards the goal of the comprehensive good for man, Muñoz developed into his concept of the "integral liberty"[26] of man. He defined integral liberty as

> freedom in all its aspects, instead of only some: freedom from fear of hunger . . . from fear of insecurity . . . from fear of the suppression of the liberties of individuals and households.[27]

Muñoz recognized a negative and a positive kind of freedom. Let us consider, then, some dimensions that come into play when we speak of "freedom." At times we may mean a negative sense of freedom, as when we speak of *freedom-from* some adverse circumstance as, for instance, a set of chains. At other times we may emphasize a positive sense of freedom, as when we speak of *freedom-to* achieve something that seems good to us, and which may really be good in itself. That it be really and not just apparently good depends, of course, on whether it promotes our authentic fulfillment as persons and harmonizes with our end as human beings. Now the end we have as human beings is not chosen by us, but is given to us by nature. As the end of the apple tree is to bear apples, so the mission of the rational being is to lead a life in accordance with reason. This is why the view of freedom which depicts it as a total absence of causes or indeterminism is inadequate, since the human will *is* subject to a cause, namely, the causality of the natural end of man, which is his personal fulfillment or what is known as "happiness." Aristotle observed that men always act in light of some good.[28] Plato recognized that all rational agents deeply desire to be happy.[29] This means that the will or rational wish is oriented by nature towards happiness or the highest good.

Out of this natural orientation of the will emerges the freedom of man, for the will, being fundamentally committed to the highest good, remains basically indifferent to all other things that are not the highest good. According to Thomistic philosophy, it is because the will is pledged essentially to the highest good, that *it is pledged to nothing else* and is therefore free.[30] Nothing short of the highest good satisfies the will. This is why things that fall short of the highest good do not constrain the will; they may be more or less desirable only to the extent that they participate in and lead to the good. Though the will is determined a priori by its natural end, which is the good, it is in no way determined by the means that lead to that end. Faced with different means, the will remains free to choose or reject them, to act or not to act regarding them, to prefer one over the other. It is not, then, a question of indeterminism. On the contrary, thanks to the determining causality of man's natural end, we have the capacity to act or not to act in the face of all other things and thus to be masters of our choices and decisions. Freedom is precisely this mastery that the will has over means because it is not determined by them but only by the final end. To distinguish it from indeterminism, let us call freedom thus conceived "autonomy." And since it is given to us by our very nature let us call it *initial autonomy*.

Positive or negative, that is, whether it seeks what is appropriate or shuns what is not appropriate, freedom is always exercised, consciously or unconsciously, for the sake of happiness. Now when the will is successful in its choices and decisions, that is, when it chooses means that actually lead to the good, and furthermore, when through the repetition of right choices the latter become settled into habits that define character—which will henceforth produce only right choices—we acquire then a stable disposition more committed and akin to the good, which is known as "virtue." The freedom of initial autonomy still persists, but it has become virtuous for it has appropriated and internalized those means, requirements, demands, laws or principles that actually lead to the good. Operating now closer to its own natural end, initial autonomy has fulfilled itself. This is why this synthesis of freedom and law could be called *ultimate autonomy*.

Initial autonomy, also known as free will, self-direction, or self-government, which is the opposite of extraneous or superfluous government, is not blind nor arbitrary, but aims by nature at becoming ultimate autonomy. If happiness is the natural end of action, and if happiness consists in the wise employment of freedom to achieve material and spiritual goods that complete or perfect life, the misuse of freedom amounts to its corruption. A person who errs, for example—whether through ignorance, weakness, vice, wickedness or bad luck—is really less autonomous than one who finds his way to fulfillment, because the latter, and not the former, has accomplished the natural end of autonomy, which is the attainment of the good.

The phenomenon of liberty, which I have briefly described in Thomistic terms, not only manifests itself in the life of particular persons, but also in the life of collective persons or communities, including what Muñoz called "la patria-pueblo" (the homeland-people).[31] Muñoz thought, for example, that freedom is no mere optionality or arbitrariness, but is oriented towards a given end. He always insisted that the given end of a nation is not necessarily its formal "independence," because the natural end of a people is not to have this or that political status but rather to use the one it has, or to create the status that better suits its purpose, which is to achieve "a great civilization."[32] To prove his point Muñoz observed—in his speech at the Hotel San Juan on 19 February 1961—that there are peoples, like those of Cuba or Mississippi, who enjoy a traditional political status, but which nevertheless fall short of realizing the ideal of liberty and great civilization. The end of civilization is, for Muñoz, the formation of a fully educated people moved by lofty inspirations beyond the drive for acquisition and living in a society "where no one is less than what God intended him to be."[33]

The fulfillment of the economic and political ideals should free man to realize the cultural ideal or "the good life," the life of culture and contemplation. Thus all men should be freed *from* hunger, extreme poverty, ill health, ignorance, and hopelessness, and all should equally be freed *from* such man-made perversions as slavery, colonialism, and oppression, *in order to* be able to lead a noble life. The economic and the political ideals are not final ends but rather "intermediate goals," that is, things which possess enough intrinsic goodness to be considered as ends but which are also means towards even higher ends. Man must use his free will to attain the economic and political ideals, because they themselves are part of happiness and because they allow for the development of the spiritual nature of man as another essential component of the good for man. Economic and political ideals are to the overall good of man, what economic and political freedom are to his integral freedom: the former are ingredients of the good, while the latter are components of authentic human freedom as it aims towards the good. The good for Puerto Rico, as envisioned by Muñoz, consists of achieving both economic and political freedom, freedom-from poverty and colonialism, which would free-man-to lead the good life. In other words, Muñoz aimed at integral freedom and the good for Puerto Rico as a human community.

NOTES

5. Luis Muñoz Marín, Speech delivered in Barranquitas, Puerto Rico on 17 July 1963. My translation.

6. Within the Thomistic tradition, man considered as a chunk of matter or as an animal is just one more *individual*, that is, a mere part of the cosmic landscape, as Jacques Maritain puts it: "a fragment of a species, a part of the universe, a unique point in the immense web of cosmic, ethnical, historical forces and influences—and bound by their laws" (Jacques Maritain, *The Person and the Common Good*, trans. John J. Fitzgerald [London: Geoffrey Bles, 1948], 27); but man as synthesis of the two principles of matter and spirit, of the temporal and the eternal, is a *person*, that is, a unique individual possessed of rationality, freedom, and supratemporal dignity.

7. Luis Muñoz Marín, *Mensajes al pueblo puertorriqueño*, with an introduction by Antonio J. Colorado (San Juan: Inter American University Press, 1980), 9. My translation.

8. Luis Muñoz Marín, Inaugural address delivered in San Juan on 2 January 1953. My translation.

9. Ibid.

10. Luis Muñoz Marín, "La personalidad puertorriqueña en el Estado Libre Asociado," Speech delivered at the *Asamblea General de la Asociación de Maestros* de Puerto Rico on 29 December 1953. My translation.

11. Muñoz Marín, Inaugural address delivered in San Juan on 2 January 1953.

12. Ibid.

13. Ibid.

14. Muñoz strove, with the Popular Democratic Party, to realize the economic, political, and cultural ideals respectively through Operation Bootstrap, Operation Commonwealth, and Operation Serenity.

15. Muñoz Marín, Inaugural address delivered in San Juan on 2 January 1953.

16. Ibid.

17. Luis Muñoz Marín, *Discursos oficiales*, vol. 1 of *Los gobernadores electos de Puerto Rico* (Río Piedras: Corporación de Servicios Bibliotecarios, 1973), 375. My translation.

18. Luis Muñoz Marín, *Memorias: autobiografía pública (1940-1952)*, with an Introduction by Jaime Benítez (San Germán: Inter American University of Puerto Rico, 1992), xi.

19. Muñoz Marín, Inaugural address delivered in San Juan on 2 January 1953.

20. Muñoz Marín, *Discursos oficiales*, 375.

21. Luis Muñoz Marín, "Cultura y democracia," Speech delivered at the *Foro del Ateneo Puertorriqueño* in San Juan on 1940. My translation.

22. Luis Muñoz Marín, Speech delivered at the Rotary Club on 19 June 1956; "Del tiempo de Muñoz Rivera a nuestro tiempo," Speech delivered on 17 July 1956; *Mensajes al pueblo*, 324.

23. Luis Muñoz Marín, Speech delivered on the occasion of the first anniversary of the Commonwealth of Puerto Rico in San Juan on 25 July 1953. My translation.

24. Luis Muñoz Marín, Notes for a speech delivered at the Rotary Club of San Juan on 28 July 1953. My translation.

25. Luis Muñoz Marín, "Development Through Democracy," *The Annals of the American Academy of Political and Social Science* 285 (1953): 6.

26. Luis Muñoz Marín, Speech delivered in Barranquitas on 17 July 1951. My translation. See also *Discursos*, 6-9, 267, 330, 465; *Mensajes*, 32, 58.

27. Ibid.

28. Aristotle *Nicomachean Ethics* 1094a1.

29. Plato *Meno* 77b-78b.

30. Aquinas *Summa Contra Gentiles* I.82; John of St. Thomas *Cursus Philosophicus, Naturalis Philosophiae* IV.12.2; Yves R. Simon, *Freedom of Choice* (New York: Fordham University Press, 1969), 102-106; Jacques Maritain, *Du régime temporel et de la liberté* (Paris: Desclée de Brouwer et Cie., 1933), 8-11.

31. Muñoz Marín, Speech delivered in Barranquitas, Puerto Rico on 17 July 1951.

32. Luis Muñoz Marín, Speech delivered on the occasion of an homage paid to Muñoz at the Hotel San Juan in Isla Verde, Puerto Rico on 19 February 1961.

33. Luis Muñoz Marín, Speech delivered at the *Asamblea General de la Asociación de Maestros* in San Juan on 28 December 1962. My translation.

CHAPTER 2

MUÑOZ'S CRITIQUE OF INDEPENDENCE FOR PUERTO RICO

The decolonization of Puerto Rico, necessary for its political freedom, was an aspect of its political ideal. In Muñoz's day, three status options were traditionally debated in Puerto Rico: independence, statehood, and autonomy, or, in other words, separation, annexation, and free association. In his youth, Muñoz favored independence, because he thought that independence and freedom were one and the same. But he later left behind what he came to realize was too simplistic a notion. In a speech delivered in Maricao, Puerto Rico, in 1952, Muñoz illustrated the fallacy of equating freedom and independence through an analogy with the fictional character Robinson Crusoe. In Muñoz's version, the shipwrecked sailor thought that he was the freest man in the world, because he was alone on an island where he had to answer to no one except himself. But when he felt the need for the basic provisions of life, like food, clothing and shelter, it took him a long time and great effort to acquire them. Muñoz concluded that Robinson Crusoe might have been the most "independent" man alive but was certainly not "free." Robinson Crusoe, shackled by his physical needs as well as by his isolation and aloneness, did not have the economic freedom that would enable him to live a noble life. Muñoz argued that, similarly, in the case of Puerto Rico, independence would have brought about the exclusion of the island from the free market with the United States, and this would have amounted to utter desolation for the already poverty-stricken country. According to Muñoz, Puerto Rico would have then been enslaved by the hopelessness of not being able to improve its condition of extreme poverty. Puerto Rico would also have had to face separation from the United States, from cooperating people who could lend a helping hand. The ideal of independence for Puerto Rico, in neglecting one aspect of integral liberty, namely, economic freedom, revealed itself to be a false means that would fall short of attaining the goal. Muñoz concluded that independence was economically impossible for Puerto Rico; therefore it was not a genuine (i.e., effective) means to achieve the good.

According to Muñoz's speech in Maricao, the *Independentistas* neglected economics in their search for political freedom, because they were convinced—as he was during his youth—that the only form of political freedom was independence. Since the separatists thought that the alternatives to independence (which they equated with freedom) were either total assimilation to the United States as a state, or the indignity of colonialism, they concluded that independence was the only patriotic path to follow. But Muñoz realized that the identification of independence and freedom is an arbitrary axiom not founded on any natural or man-made law. The word "independence," he argued, is clearly not synonymous with the word "freedom."[34] On the contrary, Muñoz perceived that, in the particular case of the Puerto Rico of his day, independence would actually have diminished real liberty:

> Nothing could enslave us more than handicapping our great drive towards a happy future with

a rigid, obsolescent, unprogressive, or inapplicable status formula."[35]

Muñoz could not believe that independence was the only formula that could achieve political freedom. He thought that this certainly could not be the case in the 20th century, considering that human creativity is not limited to such fields as art, science, and technology, but also manifests itself in the political realm. He contended that man can surely invent a variety of forms to achieve genuine political liberation, and should not be limited by dogmatic prejudices: "Peoples are the creators of political formulas," he said, "and not their slaves."[36]

According to Muñoz, independence advocates were limited by the 19th century concept of the "national state."[37] He traced the origin of this concept to the notion of the "sovereignty" of kings in past centuries, which became that of "freedom" when transposed from kingships to peoples. He argued that, while nationalism was helpful in producing cohesion among the people against their feudal lords, "for the larger task now confronting mankind the national idea—the sovereign-nation-state—is obsolescent."[38] In the modern world it has become clear that no nation is really "independent" in the nationalist sense; there was a time when the economy and defense could be exclusively national, but not today. According to Muñoz, the country that most nearly approaches this kind of independence is the United States of America, but even it cannot survive with a self-contained economy. And since no modern country, including the United States, can be adequately defended militarily from within its own boundaries, Muñoz critically reexamined the old-fashioned concept of absolute "sovereignty":

We are confronted with a fact, simple in itself, although still obscure to many: sovereignty, in the ponderous sense of its poor but proud semantics, is not only unnecessary to freedom, but worship-

ing sovereignty may be positively inimical to freedom.[39]

*   *   *

If maintained rigidly, the principle of sovereignty . . . becomes a kind of juridical wild beast,
impeding the path of liberty which must now be
founded on new forms of associations between
peoples.[40]

If no country is complete, autonomous, or independent in
the sense of self-sufficient, then Muñoz is right in claiming that
freedom today calls for broad and encompassing associations.
Muñoz did recognize independence as one form of political freedom, but not as the only one and decidedly not the one for
Puerto Rico. While he granted that the separatists were right in
emphasizing that man must be freed from colonialism, he thought
they were mistaken in assuming that there was one and only one
way of achieving this, a way that, in the case of the Puerto Rico
of his day, sacrificed all hope for a better future. Muñoz firmly
believed that independence in the broad sense of political freedom and mastery over genuine (i.e., effective) means to the Good,
that is, independence in the sense of "autonomy" or integral liberty,[41] could be achieved without the need of to break all ties
with those things that actually strengthen and perfect freedom.
He always stressed that Puerto Rico chose to be associated with
the United States not because it despises freedom but, on the
contrary, because Puerto Ricans believe that "there is more freedom in broad association than in petty isolation."[42] Muñoz
thought, for example, that in its association with the United States,
Puerto Rico becomes part of the largest independence in the
world. The American flag, he claimed, completes real liberty in
Puerto Rico, which may be said to enjoy two independences: its
own relative independence and the independence of the United
States.[43]

Besides failing to distinguish between independence and freedom, the *independentistas* committed the further mistake of considering the formula of independence as an end in itself, instead of as a means of achieving the Good.[44] According to Muñoz, the root of these two mistakes could be traced to their rationalistic, legalistic conception of the *patria* (the homeland). Muñoz affirmed that the *independentista* concept of the homeland was not that of a human community, but that of a "national state." Logically, if one equates the homeland with "the narrow and petty concept of the national state,"[45] it follows that its independence becomes its final end. It amounts to a tautology to say that the final end of an "independent republic" (i.e., a national state) is its independence. But Muñoz criticized the nationalists for seeing the people as a "juridical entity"[46] instead of as a human community. Puerto Rico is not, he stressed, a legal-political construct, but a human community of flesh and blood. Therefore its genuine freedom is not so much a topic of juridical disquisition as a reality experienced by every man in his daily life, in his work, in his soul. Muñoz insisted that the final end of a human community is not its political status in general, nor its formal "independence" in particular, but its common good and the realization of its ideals. For him the *independentistas* confused means and ends, because they moved in a world of abstractions. Equating the homeland with the construct of the "independent republic," and "freedom" with "independence," led them to the extremist position of neglecting economic freedom for the sake of an abstract "ideal" which is not based on the real end of the community, and which is thus false, not genuine.

For Muñoz the ideal of independence was also unrealistic in that it went counter to the historical tendency of Puerto Ricans to be non-isolationist and non-nationalist.[47] In the Godkin Lectures delivered at Harvard in 1959, Muñoz pointed out that neither under the Spanish crown nor under the American flag did the people of Puerto Rico favor total separation. Historically, the overwhelming majority of the islanders supported some kind of tie or association with the metropolis. Some form or other of *autonomism* has always been the ideology of the Puerto Rican people. Hence Muñoz considered insistence on separation for the island as anti-historical.

Puerto Ricans, Muñoz said, are proud of their identity and nationality but without the narrow isolationism of nationalism. Puerto Ricans are also dead set against all kinds of colonialism—indeed, they have tenaciously striven to liberate themselves from it—but not at the cost of enslavement under other kinds of misery. Muñoz understood these traits of the Puerto Rican people and learned from them: Puerto Ricans, he realized, are both non-isolationist and anti-colonialist. Muñoz observed in the Godkin Lectures that in this nuclear world the barriers that separate man may cause his extinction. He warned of the vital need of mankind to expand the federalist principle to its maximum, so as to encompass a united world without destroying particular cultures. He favored the idea of a world government in which each country could preserve its own culture and nationality without letting the latter degenerate into nationalism or isolationism. Muñoz supported the establishment of

> a supranational executive power obeyed by all, but only in regard to a few important things. And plenty of local self-government in regard to most things. For you see, we need to be diverse and richly plural if we are to be as good and valuable to ourselves as we no doubt aspire to be.[48]

Nationalities, he thought, should enrich the world with variety and not poison it with prejudice or suspicion.

In sum, Muñoz considered independence as too narrow for Puerto Rico in many respects. Firstly, its supporters tended to have an abstract appreciation of the homeland, which they viewed as a "sovereign state," whereas in the modern world we must beware precisely of confusing the two notions. Secondly, due to this misconception, the separatists fallaciously equated the "independence" of the national-state-construct with "freedom," instead of viewing liberty as mastery, the community has in fact to choose among genuine means that lead to its given end. Under Puerto Rico's particular conditions at the time, independence "would not be independence but destruction, slavery to misery."[49] Thirdly, the *independentistas* considered independence not as a means to be evaluated by the human community, but as the final end of a legal construct. Fourthly, the separatists disregarded economic freedom and hence failed to do justice to the integral freedom of man, which is essential to the common good. Fifthly, the independence movement thrived on an obsolescent nationalism which not only forgot that union makes for strength, but also obviated the historical and cultural fact that Puerto Ricans were never a nationalist or isolationist people but preferred to form part of wider wholes to complement and expand their horizons. Believing in freedom more than in "sovereignty," the great mass of the people of Puerto Rico "wants the broad brotherhood with its fellow citizens of the United States, with all men on Earth, rather than the bitter narrowness of separatism."[50]

Puerto Ricans, Muñoz affirmed, feel pride in and affection for American citizenship with which they have lived for over 70 years, and which they have defended in war and honored in peace. Muñoz saw no reason whatsoever for separating the peoples of Puerto Rico and the United States as they have developed a genuine friendship brought about by history and an enhanced sharing of the values of religion, justice and democracy. American citizenship does not make one less of a Puerto Rican, it does not subtract anything from Puerto Rican character, on the contrary, Muñoz thought that, besides being a Puerto Rican citizen, a man can *also* be an American citizen and have two flags, both of which guarantee his liberty and individual rights:

> If we could call independence the better name of
> political freedom, then, what we feel when we see
> our flag alongside that of the United States is in-

dependence without separatism, nationality without nationalism. Because to feel nationality in fraternity with others is worthier of human quality than feeling it as a vehicle of rancor, as violence in one's soul, as a circle of fire in which one encloses, isolates, and burns oneself. Union frees, whereas isolation diminishes liberty.[51]

In the first chapter, the Thomistic doctrine was discussed, the perfection of freedom, that is, "ultimate autonomy," consists of the appropriation or internalization of the means, laws or principles that actually lead to the Good. Once the requirements of the good are recognized, not to appropriate them becomes, far from a genuine struggle for emancipation, a sign of irresponsible rebellion: "We would be like a vessel whose crew refused to examine the maps, the winds, currents, shallows, and even the nature of the sea and geography itself."[52] In the case of Puerto Rico, should there be less autonomy, that is, less power through the ballot box, less integral freedom, less mastery of real means towards authentic ends, in separation or annexation than in association with the United States, so that, to insist on the former would be to place abstract constructs over the common good. Now to alienate oneself from the common good is to alienate freedom from its given end, which amounts to depriving it of its true nature. This was precisely Muñoz's contention. According to him the *independentistas* never took independence as one means among others but rather hypostatized it into an abstract final end. They were thus mastered by a means rather than the masters of it, and hence were not free to deal with the integral liberation of Puerto Rico in its concrete historical reality. Furthermore, they were mastered by a means that was not even (in the case of Puerto Rico in those days) a genuine means, because it did not lead to integral freedom and the good. In this other sense, too, and ironically, the separatists were not free, because to choose false means that do not lead to the appropriate end betrays a lack of autonomy as the perfection of freedom.[53]

The only freedom the *independentistas* seemed to claim for Puerto Rico was a certain *freedom-from* the federal jurisdiction of the United States. But Muñoz argued that this again was illusory, because federal jurisdiction could hardly be considered an obstacle one had to be freed-from; on the contrary, most of the federal laws that applied to Puerto Rico (at first unilaterally but later through the generic consent of the Puerto Rican people) were beneficial, indeed, vital for, the island. So this illusory *freedom-from* was really a mere indeterminateness,[54] "la yola al garete" (a boat adrift), as Muñoz put it:

> What in Puerto Rico was a deadly thing was the concept of separatism: separate independence, independence without union, a boat adrift by herself in the stormy sea.[55]

The *independentistas* forgot that negative *freedom-from* only makes sense within the context of positive *freedom-to*.[56] Only when one is on the right track towards the good, can one encounter obstacles that impede the attainment of the good, which is why they are called "obstacles." One must then free oneself *from* them. But the *independentistas*, by erroneously identifying freedom with independence, divorced political from economic liberty and thus disrupted achievement of the integral liberty of man, which alone is genuine *freedom-to* attain the good. Hence independence did not represent any gain in autonomy for Puerto Rico; on the contrary, it meant the loss of the greater freedom for the island of belonging to a wider whole, one that expands its political, social and cultural horizons even while making economic freedom possible. All in all, independence represented a dramatic loss of autonomy (integral freedom) for Puerto Rico. For this reason, Muñoz discarded it as a possible solution to the problem of political status, as part of the search for the political ideal.

NOTES

34. Luis Muñoz Marín, "Significación del Estado Libre Asociado de Puerto Rico en la Unión americana," Speech delivered at the Annual Assembly of the Chamber of Commerce of Puerto Rico in San Juan on 14 February 1958. My translation.

35. Muñoz Marín, "Development through Democracy," 6.

36. Luis Muñoz Marín, "Puerto Rico Does Not Want to Be a State," *The New York Times Magazine*, 16 August 1959, 19.

37. Muñoz Marín, Speech delivered in Barranquitas on 17 July 1951.

38. Luis Muñoz Marín, "Breakthrough from Nationalism: A Small Island Looks at Big Trouble," the *Godkin Lectures* given at Harvard University, Cambridge, Mass., on 28-30 April 1959, Lecture I. See also his speech delivered at the National Press Club in Washington, D.C. on 18 June 1957.

39. Luis Muñoz Marín, Address delivered at Bate College in Maine on 9 June 1957.

40. Luis Muñoz Marín, English translation of the address delivered on the occasion of the fifth anniversary of the Commonwealth of Puerto Rico on 25 July 1957.

41. See Chapter 1.

42. Luis Muñoz Marín, "The Political Status of Puerto Rico," English translation of a speech delivered on 12 November 1954.

43. Luis Muñoz Marín, "The Deep Significance of United States Citizenship," English translation of the address delivered on the occasion of the fourth anniversary of the Commonwealth of Puerto Rico on 25 July 1956; Speech delivered at the *Asamblea del Parque Sixto Escobar* in San Juan on 24 August 1952.

44. Luis Muñoz Marín, Speech delivered at the *Asociación de Alcaldes* in San Juan on 1959; Speech delivered on the occasion of an homage paid to Muñoz at the Hotel San Juan in Isla Verde, Puerto Rico on 19 February 1961; *Discursos*, 284.

45. Muñoz Marín, "Breakthrough from Nationalism," Lecture III.

46. Luis Muñoz Marín, *Memorias: autobiografía pública 1898-1940*, with an introduction by Jaime Benítez (San Juan: Inter American University Press, 1982), 76. My translation.

47. Luis Muñoz Marín, *Puerto Rico y los Estados Unidos: su futuro en común* (San Juan: Editorial del Departamento de Instrucción Pública, 1954), 10; "The Political Status of Puerto Rico," Speech delivered on 12 November 1954.

48. Muñoz Marín, "Breakthrough from Nationalism," Lecture I.

49. Muñoz Marín, Speech delivered in Barranquitas on 17 July 1951.

50. Ibid.

51. Muñoz Marín, Speech delivered at the *Asamblea del Parque*

Sixto Escobar in San Juan on 24 August 1952. My translation.

52. Muñoz Marín, *Memorias (1940-1952)*, 365.

53. See Chapter 1.

54. See Chapter 1.

55. Luis Muñoz Marín, Speech delivered in Maricao, Puerto Rico on 17 September 1952. My translation.

56. See Chapter 1.

CHAPTER 3

MUÑOZ'S CRITIQUE OF
STATEHOOD FOR PUERTO RICO

The other status option traditionally favored by many Puerto Ricans is statehood: they want Puerto Rico to become a federated state of the American Union. Some of them want this at all costs, including the loss of their native tongue and culture; most of them think they can be a federated state without losing these important values.

Muñoz observed that, like the *independentistas*, statehooders assumed that there are only two possible ways of decolonizing Puerto Rico, namely, independence and statehood. In addition, says Muñoz, they were convinced that there is one and only one dignified way of forming part of the American Union, namely, statehood.[57] Since they did not want separation from the United States, they concluded that Puerto Rico should have been decolonized by way of becoming a federated state.

According to Muñoz, this line of reasoning reveals less imagination than Congress had shown when, right after the Treaty of Paris, it decided that Puerto Rico should not become a typical possession. In the second of the Godkin Lectures Muñoz narrates how Congress concluded that the Union should accommodate Puerto Rico as an "unincorporated" rather than "incorporated" territory (as they had other possessions), because under the latter status Puerto Rico would have been subject to a uniform application of the Constitution, including taxation laws, as happens with all states and incorporated territories of the United States. But Congress realized that the "poorhouse of the Caribbean," as the island was known at the time, simply could not pay federal taxes. So they turned to a new status, the "unincorporated territory," to accommodate Puerto Rico in a way that would exempt it from paying taxes.

Muñoz makes reference to this historical feat by Congress as he advances a first criticism of the annexationist movement: statehood is economically impossible. The "overwhelmingly impossible"[58] burden of taxes would have produced as great a disaster as independence would with its exclusion of the island from the free market with the United States. Muñoz confessed that he did not exactly like to advance the economic argument, since he was the first to admit that politics is much more than mere economics. Yet he said that the economic argument had to be stated, because it was a decisive one. In "El status político de Puerto Rico," a speech delivered on 4 June 1959, Muñoz observes that, under statehood, Puerto Ricans would have to pay federal taxes in addition to local taxes.[59] The latter could not be eliminated, since that would amount to reducing public works and services drastically and neglecting the economic ideal altogether. Moreover, under statehood the fiscal autonomy that allows Puerto Rico to grant tax exemptions would terminate, putting an end to the incentive that attracts many American and other companies to establish plants on the island. These factories were vital to the industrialization of the island, and Muñoz quoted economic studies which concluded that their closing would mean economic disaster for Puerto Rico.[60] Muñoz observed that the mere talk of statehood adversely affected the economy by scaring away potential investors.

According to Muñoz, statehooders failed to recognize these facts, because they were trapped in the "intellectual strait jacket"[61] of the independence-statehood dichotomy according to which there are two and only two dignified solutions to the political status issue. Any other status besides independence or statehood was, for them, second class colonialism. Statehood, like independence, aimed at freedom from colonialism and, unlike independence, it advocated forming part of the wider political system of the United States. But like independence it could only be obtained at the expense of the economic freedom, and hence the integral freedom, of the islanders. Muñoz contended that a political freedom that sacrifices integral liberty is an illusory freedom, a freedom of form rather than substance.

Some statehooders claimed that, as a state, the sum going to federal taxes would be compensated by an increase in federal aid. Muñoz said that this was not what the economic studies revealed.[62] He argued further that, even if that alleged scenario were mathematically accurate, it implied the conversion of Puerto Rico into an "estado limosnero" (a beggar state).[63] Speaking before the Constitutional Convention on 26 December 1951, Muñoz explained that, as a "beggar state" not only would Puerto Rico's economy collapse, but the island would not have the freedom to use its economic resources as it saw fit. Supposing—though Muñoz said that this was not the case—that the state of Puerto Rico received the same amount of money it paid in federal taxes in the form of an increase in aid. It would then have to use that additional aid money in the way the Federal government required and not in the way the local legislature considered best. With the aid money Puerto Rico cannot undertake the public works it does with the revenue it collects locally *all of which stays in Puerto Rico thanks to its fiscal autonomy*. This brings us to another of Muñoz's arguments against statehood: besides the loss of economic freedom, there would also be a loss of political freedom.[64] The economic resources would then be governed from Washington, and the local legislature would not be free to use available funds in whatever ways it deemed necessary for the solution of those problems that directly affect the citizens of Puerto Rico. According to Muñoz, this loss of fiscal and political autonomy would entail a loss of efficiency in government, since the islanders would not be able to face Puerto Rican problems with Puerto Rican solutions. But worse than a loss of efficiency, the loss of autonomy means that the votes of the citizens would have less effect in the realization of their ideals, which, according to Muñoz, amounts to a setback in democracy.

In his message addressed to the people of Puerto Rico on 19 August 1962, Muñoz observed that, not only would taxation laws apply uniformly, but so would other federal legislation that under autonomy may or may not apply, or apply flexibly, but under statehood would *have* to apply to Puerto Rico. With regard to these laws there would also be a centralization of powers and a loss of autonomy.

Another loss of autonomy under statehood pointed out by Muñoz follows from the fact that, once Puerto Rico became a state it would forever remain a state. According to Muñoz, the states have sealed their destiny within the union through the Constitution and the Civil War.[65] While he conceived of Commonwealth status as permanent and final in nature, he thought that, in principle at least, it allowed the citizens to exchange it for another status like statehood or independence. Though the possibility of making wrong choices indicates a lack of freedom (because the will is not yet in complete harmony with the Good),[66] and though in Muñoz's time independence and statehood would have been extremely bad choices, Muñoz was open to the possibility that there could come a time when these formulas would turn into genuine options, a time, for example, when they would not entail the destruction of the economic ideal. In his speech delivered in Barranquitas on 17 July 1950, Muñoz reasoned that if that time came, having more genuine choices would enhance liberty. Of course, Muñoz held that even if Puerto Rico were economically strong enough either to pay taxes as a state or be independent, he would still prefer the Commonwealth because of the "moral values"[67] he saw in it. Though Muñoz had no major theoretical objections to independence if people should ever want it, he eventually came to the conclusion that statehood would *never* be a genuine option for Puerto Rico for economic and cultural reasons.[68]

Muñoz also observed in his speech before the Rotary Club of Santurce on 12 November 1958 that, as an autonomous body politic, Puerto Rico can make modifications and improvements to its permanent relationship with the United States through direct negotiations with Congress in the way of bilateral agreements, while a federated state has to convince two thirds of Congress and three fourths of the legislatures of all the states to accomplish that. Furthermore, though Puerto Rico follows the leadership of the United States in foreign affairs, the island has more flexibility than a state to engage in international relations. It has, for example, its own Olympic committee and has been very successful in international sports. In sum, for Muñoz federated statehood would represent a grave loss of economic and political freedom for Puerto Rico.

Statehood does seem to offer a certain autonomy in the sense of self-government through more participation in the federal sphere. As a Commonwealth Puerto Rico has only a Resident Commissioner with no vote in Congress, and its citizens do not vote for the president, while as a state Puerto Rico would have voting congressmen and the presidential vote. But according to Muñoz, two senators and six representatives, plus the presidential vote, would not add any real power to the votes of Puerto Ricans on election day. He argued that the influence in Congress of two senators and six representatives among so many others would be dissolved like a drop of angostura in a Martini cocktail.[69] Even supposing that they did in fact represent an increase in autonomy—which Muñoz denied—this again would be at the expense of a greater autonomy in the economic, political, and cultural spheres. For example, two senators and six representatives would not be able to achieve vital fiscal autonomy, with its many advantages for Puerto Rico, or protect Puerto Rico's Spanish heritage. Again, statehood would give Puerto Ricans the right to vote for the president, but overnight they would become "a minority"[70] in their own land. According to Muñoz, the power of the vote of each Puerto Rican, his influence on government, and thus his control over his own destiny and affairs would ultimately be impaired under statehood. He stressed that though Puerto Rico does not have voting congressmen, it does have voting citizens who approved the Commonwealth relationship with its dynamic potential for growth. This relationship has the flexibility, he said, to seek forms of participation that would be congenial in Puerto Rico's particular circumstances. In his message to Puerto Ricans on 19 August 1962, he claimed that Congress and the people of Puerto Rico can agree on avenues of participation other than voting congressmen and the presidential vote. But to insist on becoming a state just to imitate the kind of participation characteristic of the states would be, for Muñoz, to offer a remedy worse than the illness. Participation is nothing but a form of autonomy or self-government: "the participation of Puerto Rico in the Federal Congress is different from that of the states in exchange for a *much greater liberty* in internal affairs."[71] According to Muñoz, the capacity to influence the general politics of the United States through voting congressmen and the presidential vote would amount on the whole to less autonomy for Puerto Rico than if the latter had complete authority, within the terms of the association, over its own politics. He contended that, given the choice, Puerto Rico would prefer the latter.[72]

In "El status político de Puerto Rico," a speech delivered on 3 June 1959, as well as in his message of 19 August 1962, Muñoz explained that, in contrast with the case of Puerto Rico, statehood represented a gain and not a loss of political autonomy for other territories of the United States. He observed that these other possessions never had the autonomy of an "unincorporated territory" but started as "incorporated territories," paying taxes—which they could afford—so that their passage into statehood did not mean a loss but, on the contrary, a gain in political autonomy (i.e., through their decolonization). But Muñoz understood that for Puerto Rico to follow the same road would mean passage from an "unincorporated territory 's" status, free from uniform taxation laws, to the status of a state without this freedom from a heavy burden. It would also mean the transition from a more autonomous legislature to a less autonomous one. Statehood meant centralization instead of decentralization of powers.

According to Yves R. Simon (1903-1961), the great contemporary political philosopher, societies elect governing bodies to take charge of the demands of the common good *so that* the private citizens, freed from that responsibility, can concentrate on the pursuit of their particular good. Thus the *raison d'être* of government is, for Simon, to preserve and promote the autonomy of particular citizens. Simon argues that, since personal freedom is an absolute value and the "glory of the rational nature,"[73] natural law demands that it be cultivated, the legitimacy of a regime depending precisely on whether or not it fulfills this purpose. This is why Simon considers democracy to be a superior form of government. Democracy, as the political form that allows the governed actually to step into the governing process, not only opposes centralization of power, but deliberately promotes decentralization. Not only does it preserve the autonomy of citizens and of subsidiary social units, but *maximizes* it, so that government is truly for the people, of the people, and by the people. The people govern themselves, in other words, they are autonomous. If the preservation of autonomy is the core of political justice or the condition of the legitimacy of a government, we can say that the maximization of autonomy is the heart of democracy.

Since progress toward autonomy is more than a mere policy issue; it is an element of natural law. So statehood for Puerto Rico would constitute a political injustice, namely, the passage from a status of greater autonomy to one of less autonomy. And if the maximization of autonomy is the heart of democracy, it must also be concluded that statehood for Puerto Rico would be at odds with the genuine spirit of democracy.

While Muñoz never suggested that statehood as such was undemocratic, he insisted that in the case of Puerto Rico it does represent a loss of liberty. Muñoz made it clear that this fact does not indicate any deficiency on the part of the American political system. On the contrary, he held that the case of Puerto Rico shows the rich potential of the Constitution and American democracy. According to Muñoz, the case of Puerto Rico demonstrates that the American federal system is not bound by "legalisms"[74] or "mean interpretations"[75] to states and incorporated territories, but can also accommodate, for example, an "unincorporated territory" that may later become an "associated (e.g., non-federated) state," as is the case of Puerto Rico. This historical fact, Muñoz thought, presents the American constitution as vital and rich, besides proving that the principles of federalism and of self-determination of peoples were not exhausted by the formula of statehood as designed by the original thirteen American colonies. Speaking before the Constitutional Convention on 26 December 1951, Muñoz applauded the creative feat of the original thirteen colonies and the fact that the fifty states belong to the union in a uniform fashion. But he thought that that feat did not exhaust political creativity and that the vital American federation had the possibility of receiving a state that could join in in an equally dignified though dissimilar fashion:

> The political mind cannot be limited to one sole rigid form of state in a federation as spiritually vital, as fully acquainted with the essence of human freedom, as dynamic, as the federation formed by the United States of America.[76]

Muñoz quoted the words of statesman Henry L. Stimson on 1912 defending the granting of American citizenship to Puerto Rico, as an anticipation of the possibility of a status like the Commonwealth within the American system:

> I see myself no inconsistency in the grant of American citizenship to Porto Rico; no inconsistency between that and the ultimate ideal that Porto Rico shall have practically an independent local self-government. I think that is what most of the people of the United States would prefer to have them do—that is, a relation where they exercise supervision over their own affairs, over their own fiscal and local self-government; with the link of American citizenship between the two countries as a tie, and in general such relations between the United States and Porto Rico as subsists, and as has been found perfectly workable in the case of the various self-governing portions of the territory of Great Britain—Australia, for instance, and Canada, to the mother country.[77]

Muñoz argued that, besides economic and political freedom, Puerto Rico would also lose cultural autonomy under statehood.[78] He held that if Puerto Rico became a state, it would lose the autonomy necessary, not only to progress economically and take charge of its own affairs, but also to protect and preserve its culture. Insofar as persons are oriented by nature towards the highest good, it transcends and surpasses all temporal societies. Therefore these societies, if they truly respect the dignity of persons, must recognize their own subordination to supratemporal values on which this dignity rests. Besides the natural law—including the principle of progress toward autonomy— these absolute values include, for example, the life of the spirit and contemplation, the immaterial dignity of truth and beauty. No government can legislate, for instance, that $2+2=5$, nor make a person declare that he is who he is not, or renounce the cultural heritage embodied by his community. These are truths that transcend the temporal common good, because they belong to the "common good of the intellects,"[79] the "community of minds,"[80]

14410-RIVE

minds which, like Cervantes, Aristotle, Lloréns Torres, and John Dewey, commune in the love of truth and beauty, in the life of knowledge, art, poetry, and the highest values of civilization. To ignore these truths is to sin against the dignity of the person and to impair by the same token the temporal common good, since the latter

> implies and requires recognition of the fundamental rights of persons and those of the domestic society in which the persons are more primitively engaged than in the political society.[81]

Indeed the same rights enjoyed by individual persons are shared by collective persons, beginning with the most basic and natural groups—such as the family and the nation—to which persons belong fundamentally, and ending with groups such as the civic or political community and the great associations of peoples, which are matters of convention.

Now Puerto Rico is a Latin American community which has spoken the Spanish language for about five centuries. Unlike the other states, it is a national group by itself, a distinct culture with Spanish, African, Taíno, and Latin American roots. Muñoz observed that the case of Puerto Rico represents "the only time in which the United States has received into the honorable brotherhood of its citizenship, a people as such, a mature culture as such."[82] According to Muñoz, the culture would be left unprotected under statehood, and the tendency would be towards the erosion of cultural identity and values. He believed that for a people to lose its personality is to lose its life, and that the life of a people deserves protection as does that of a man: "If it were not its instinct, it would be the duty of the people of Puerto Rico to preserve its identity, its sense of itself."[83] Puerto Rico, thought Muñoz, has the responsibility of preserving and enhancing its unique identity, which embodies supratemporal values such as language.

Muñoz emphasized that while Puerto Ricans are proud of their American citizenship, they are also proud of being Puerto Ricans; the immense majority of Puerto Ricans wish to be united permanently with the United States, and they all wish never to stop being Puerto Ricans. Muñoz observed that they are Puerto Ricans by nature and American citizens by convention; God made them Puerto Ricans and Congress, with the retroactive consent of Puerto Ricans, made them American citizens: "We are Puerto Ricans who are citizens of the United States, not citizens of the United States who have ceased being Puerto Ricans."[84] Muñoz thought that ways should always be found to harmonize the will of God with what men have democratically agreed.

In this connection, Muñoz describes the contrasting effects upon culture of statehood and political autonomy under Commonwealth status:

> When we speak of Commonwealth status and Statehood we are dealing with economics. But economics is not the only subject that concerns Puerto Rico. Puerto Ricans do not want to feel psychologically coerced into creating a certain type of civilization when their hearts and imagination foresee, establish [sic] their own view of things, their own variations on the kind of civilization they want to construct for themselves, on the kind of participation they want their people to have in their life together. In obtaining statehood, I believe that this psychological coercion would exist, for natural historical reasons. If Puerto Rico had the economic means to become a State, if it should apply for admission to the union, the problem of language would immediately arise. It is not a mere problem of grammar and rhetoric but a problem of spirit. The problem of the scale of values, of the kind of civilization the people of Puerto Rico wish

to create for themselves, would appear in subtle forms.

A people that feels coerced as to the kind of civilization they should want for themselves is not a free people, regardless of their political status.

However, in the United States there is nothing remotely like opposition to Puerto Rico, under Commonwealth, in a sincere and permanent association with the United States, having a personality of its own.[85]

Other Puerto Rican thinkers have denounced statehood for Puerto Rico as economical, political and cultural suicide:

To become a state we must submit to eventual assimilation, to the renunciation of our historical continuity, our cultural identity and our deep-rooted loyalties and values.[86]

Economically [statehood for Puerto Rico] is a disaster, and culturally it is suicide.[87]

In "La personalidad puertorriqueña en el Estado Libre Asociado," a speech delivered at the *Asamblea General de la Asociación de Maestros* in San Juan on 29 December 1953, Muñoz agreed that to add the knowledge of a second language to one's vernacular is enriching, but to substitute a second language for one's own amounts to a lessening of the freedom to be oneself. If culture and language are supratemporal values, then they are not negotiable under any political status but form part of the given end of the community. Hence it is part of natural law to preserve and enrich one's culture and language, and not to jeopardize them or leave them to chance.

Muñoz claimed that the Puerto Rican statehood movement is anti-historical, because the history of Puerto Rico has always moved in the direction of the broadening, and never of stagnating or reducing freedom:

> The people of Puerto Rico have never been advocates of the stagnation of their freedoms, much less of a reduction or a paring down of those freedoms—that is, of their right to resolve their own affairs.[88]

Indeed, Muñoz always thought that, practically speaking, statehood was not only an economic but also a political impossibility: "It is inconceivable that a dignified, self-respecting people would want *fewer* freedoms."[89]

> I cannot see how a people could ever vote for losing two thirds, or any large part, of its authority over its government, of its power to express itself democratically through its government.[90]

Furthermore:

> It is simply inconceivable that the Congress of the United States would establish a beggar state. The Congress of the United States does not authorize the entrance of a state until it is sure that its economy has grown to the point where it would not have to beg.[91]

In general, it is clear that a community that passes arbitrarily from a political status of more, to one of less, autonomy not only commits an anti-democratic deed—since it implies centralization of power—but, contradicting the principle of progress toward autonomy, it would also be violating natural law and committing, therefore, a great injustice, namely, the self-annulment, not just of a single individual, but of an entire people.

And if the smaller social unit, in yielding its powers to the larger social unit, loses or even jeopardizes a major tongue or culture, its conduct would be all the more abominable, since this would not only go against democracy and natural law, but, in neglecting the heritage of a moral and intellectual treasure, would trample upon other supratemporal values that are not negotiable in any political context. These belong to the spiritual realm on which the life and the dignity of persons rest. Other consequences of such a disintegrating action would be the loss of pragmatic efficiency both in the small social unit and in the larger communities of which it is part.

For Muñoz the unnecessary economic, political and cultural absorption of Puerto Rico by the United States would reduce the autonomy of the Commonwealth in the two senses described in the first chapter: (1) it would lead Puerto Rico astrays away from the road toward its material and spiritual self-realization (loss of ultimate autonomy), and (2) it would diminish its self-government and self-direction (loss of initial autonomy). Statehood not only does not lead to the good or integral liberty (ultimate autonomy) of Puerto Rico, but, on the contrary, destroys the necessary condition of all genuine happiness, namely, that it be reached through the exercise of one's own effort (initial autonomy). The damage suffered by Puerto Rico as the part, would make itself felt in the whole—including the United States, the Caribbean, Latin America, and the rest of the world—of which it is part.

Statehooders, considering statehood as a final end instead of as a means for achieving the common good, neglected these truths and were willing to renounce Puerto Rico's economic, political and cultural autonomy so that Washington would sustain and govern it, impairing thus the integral liberty of Puerto Ricans for the sake of a status formula. In truth, statehood represented an economy in shambles, a less autonomous legislature, less efficiency in government because of centralization (instead of decentralization) of power, an anti-historical and culturally suicidal move involving political injustice and a setback for democracy. For these reasons Muñoz discarded it as a possible solution to the problem of political status as part of the search for the political ideal.

14410-RIVE

NOTES

57. Luis Muñoz Marín, Speech delivered at the Graduation Ceremony of the *Universidad Católica de Santa María* in Ponce, Puerto Rico on 22 May 1964; *Discursos*, 343-44.

58. Muñoz Marín, "Breakthrough from Nationalism," Lecture II.

59. See also Luis Muñoz Marín, Speech delivered at the Rotary Club of Santurce on 12 November 1958; *Discursos*, 144.

60. Luis Muñoz Marín, Speech delivered at the Lions Club of San Juan on 22 July 1959; "El status político de Puerto Rico," Speech delivered on 4 June 1959.

61. Muñoz Marín, "Development Through Democracy," 4.

62. Muñoz Marín, "El status político de Puerto Rico," Speech delivered on 4 June 1959.

63. Luis Muñoz Marín, Speech delivered at the Lions Club of San Juan on 4 November 1959. My translation.

64. Luis Muñoz Marín, "Del tiempo de Muñoz Rivera a nuestro tiempo," Speech delivered on 17 July 1956. See also Muñoz Marín, English translation of a message addressed to the people of Puerto Rico on the plebiscite on 19 August 1962; *Discursos*, 345.

65. Muñoz Marín, *Discursos*, 144.

66. If my purpose is to build a house, for example, I am less free if I have the possibility of employing defective tools that can make me err in measuring, or that cannot get the job done. "Since freedom is a power of choosing the means within the limits defined by the end, any condition that puts at stake the end itself is profoundly in conflict with the very essence of freedom" (Yves R. Simon, *Freedom and Community*, ed. Charles P. O'Donnell (New York: Fordham University Press, 1968), 43. See also Aquinas *Summa Theologiae* I.62.8.ad 3; Rivera, "Political Autonomy and the Good," 25-34. See also Chapter 1.

67. Muñoz Marín, "El status político de Puerto Rico," Speech delivered on 4 June 1959; Speech delivered at the Rotary Club of Santurce on 12 November 1958. See Chapter 5.

68. Muñoz Marín, *Memorias (1940-19562)*, xi, 2.

69. Muñoz Marín, Notes for a speech delivered at the Rotary Club of San Juan on 28 July 1953. See also "El status político de Puerto Rico," Speech delivered on 3 June 1959.

70. Salvador Tió, "Aclaración a una declaración," in *Desde el tuétano* (San Juan: Editorial Cultural, 1992), 98. See also Salvador Tió, "El 'Estado-negocio'," in *Desde el tuétano*, 95.

71. Luis Muñoz Marín, "El status político: Estado Libre Asociado ó Estado Federado ó Independencia," Speech delivered on 3 June 1959. My translation. Emphasis added.

72. Muñoz Marín, *Puerto Rico y los Estados Unidos*, 15.

73. Yves R. Simon, *Nature and Functions of Authority* (Milwaukee: Marquette University Press, 1940), 44.

74. Muñoz Marín, Speech delivered on the occasion of the first anniversary of the Commonwealth in San Juan on 25 July 1953.

75. Ibid.

76. Muñoz Marín, "Significación del Estado Libre Asociado de Puerto Rico en la Unión americana," Speech delivered at the Annual Assembly of the Chamber of Commerce of Puerto Rico on 14 February 1958.

77. Muñoz Marín, "Breakthrough from Nationalism," Lecture II.

78. Muñoz Marín, Speech delivered at the Lions Club of San Juan on 22 July 1959; "The Status of Puerto Rico," Speech delivered on 12 March 1959; English translation of notes for a speech delivered at the Convention of the San Juan Popular Youth on 13 March 1960.

79. Maritain, *The Person and the Common Good*, 43-46.

80. Ibid.

81. Ibid., 36-37.

82. Luis Muñoz Marín, Speech delivered at the *Congreso Interamericano de Municipalidades* on 3 December 1954. My translation.

83. Muñoz Marín, Speech delivered at the Hotel San Juan on 19 February 1961.

84. Muñoz Marín, "The Deep Significance of United States

Citizenship," English translation of the address delivered at the fourth anniversary of the Commonwealth of Puerto Rico on 25 July 1956. American citizenship was granted to Puerto Ricans by an unilateral act of Congress on 1919, but the islanders gave their consent upon their approval of the Commonwealth relationship.

85. Muñoz Marín, English translation of notes for a speech delivered at the Convention of the San Juan Popular Youth on 13 March 1960.

86. Salvador Tió, " . . . An Another on Statehood," in *Desde el tuétano*, 84.

87. Salvador Tió, "¿La estadidad para quién?" in *Desde el tuétano*, 94. My translation.

88. Muñoz Marín, English translation of a message addressed to the people of Puerto Rico on the plebiscite on 19 August 1962.

89. Ibid.

90. Muñoz Marín, *Mensajes al pueblo*, 114. My translation.

91. Muñoz Marín, Speech delivered at the Lions Club of San Juan on 4 November 1959.

CHAPTER 4

STATEHOOD AND INDEPENDENCE AS "UTOPIAS," "IDEOLOGIES" AND "MYTHS"

Muñoz's criticisms of statehood and independence as proposed statuses for Puerto Rico pointed to the same conclusion: neither of them was a realistic option. Both were economically impossible and anti-historical, statehood being also anti-democratic and inimical to the culture.[92] None of these traditional status options resulted in a genuine means to achieve the good; on the contrary, both meant destruction for Puerto Rico and a consequent economic and political burden for the United States. It thus seemed as if Puerto Rico had nowhere to turn, because the premise assumed by many in Muñoz's time was that, apart from statehood and independence, the other alternative was the indignity of colonialism. Muñoz affirmed that under this unrealistic premise, Puerto Ricans faced the following artificial dilemma: "Would you choose to eat your bread in shame or proclaim your dignity while hungry?"[93] But he was able to substitute a more hopeful question and also to find an answer:

> If there are only two exits, and both of them kill
> you, whereas just staying where you are is humili-

ating and shameful, what to do? Look for another
exit; open a door where there is none.[94]

If the traditional formulas to solve the problem of colonial
status or a despotic regime over a territory are not applicable to
the territory's particular situation, then a new form has to be
fashioned. According to Muñoz, what Puerto Rico obviously
needed was a relationship that would allow the island to form
part of the American union without being economically, politi-
cally or culturally absorbed by it. Some kind of association with
the United States was called for that would continue Federal legislation that was vital to the island, while being flexible enough
to avoid those federal laws that were detrimental to it.

For Muñoz the question of the political status of Puerto Rico
was "uniquely determined," to use Simon's terms.[95] There was
only one choice: neither separation nor annexation, but autonomy
in free association. According to Simon, when a means is uniquely
determined, any enlightened society would recognize the right-
ness and necessity of choosing it, and all intellectually alert and
morally sound persons would unanimously choose such a means
through rational deliberation or affective intuition. Failure to do
so, he thought, would betray some kind of intellectual deficiency
such as ignorance or error, or some moral defect such as ill will or
vice.

We have seen that, among the errors that Muñoz attributed
to the annexationists and the separatists was their legalistic conception of the homeland. Both groups failed to see the homeland as a human community in a unique historical situation call-
ing for creative solutions and new ways of facing life and destiny.
Puerto Rico was for them a "colony" that had to be decolonized
by way of the two classical status options found in the textbooks,
namely, statehood or independence. These two formulas, said
Muñoz, constituted their "ideals."[96] In a speech delivered at the
Asociación de Alcaldes on 1959, he criticized extremists for not
thinking of the construction of hospitals and schools, and for

not considering hope for a better future, as legitimate ideals based on the common good of the community and participation in the general good by the people. Instead, said Muñoz, their "ideals" were circumscribed to "delivering a speech in favor of independence or . . . in favor of statehood."[97]

Another error which derived from so formalistic a conception of the homeland was that political status came to be seen as an end in itself instead of as a means towards the attainment of a great civilization. Viewing Puerto Rico as a "colony," extremists considered Statehood or Independence as final ends instead of as means. We could surmise that the reason they failed to realize that statehood and independence were not genuine means, that they did not lead to the good of the people of Puerto Rico, is precisely that they did not see them as *means* to begin with, but rather as final ends. This category mistake lead them to their cruel attempt to sacrifice a people to an idea: they wanted statehood or independence, even at the cost of the starvation of the people. This attitude is precisely what Simon understands by the "spirit of utopia":[98] there are these purely intellectual or juridical constructs (e.g., the "51st state" or the "republic" of Puerto Rico) which some people want to apply from above, so to speak, to a community, without considering whether those preconceived, rigid formulas are really applicable to the particular case in question. Since they are formulas taken out of textbooks—which no doubt have worked well for other communities but that do not necessarily apply in all cases—they may be at odds with the concrete situation of the community at hand. If so, their application turns into the imposition of an a priori abstraction for the sake of which great natural energies and life, both physical and spiritual, as well as great historical substance, in the form of culture and personality traits, are sacrificed. For Puerto Rican extremists, "statehood" or "independence" became the sole concern, and the economic and cultural ideals, in other words, the integral liberty and good of the people of Puerto Rico, were neglected. Against

the "spiritual confusion"[99] involved in such an attitude, Muñoz
wrote:

> It is unworthy . . . [and] the negation of all ide-
> als, to risk, for abstract ideas, the hope for a better
> life, the deep belief in the integral freedom of
> the . . . people.[100]

According to Muñoz, that both the annexationists and the
separatists espoused a utopian mentality, that is, one that pre-
tends to accommodate reality to political thought (including
technicisms) instead of political thought to reality, is proven by
their insistence on the arbitrary, dogmatic axiom that there are
two and only two possible, respectable ways to decide Puerto
Rico's political status: statehood or independence. This unrealistic, either/or presupposition, this "narrow and mean legalism,"[101]
clearly reflects the extreme, radical character of a rationalistic mind
thinking in black-and-white terms. Muñoz observed that the
"unimaginative, narrow . . . [and] utterly dangerous"[102] theory,
according to which there are only two forms of political freedom and that all else is second class colonialism, mastered many
minds, trapping them in the artificial dilemma of having to choose
between economic ruin under statehood and independence, on
the one hand, and political indignity, on the other.

The "51st state," for example, constitutes a utopia, because it
amounts to a formula—federated statehood—that is really inapplicable to the particular case of Puerto Rico, but that some people
insist on applying to this community from above regardless of
the costs in physical, historical, and spiritual vitality. Instead of
beginning with the concrete reality of the people in order to accommodate political thought to this reality, they begin, on the
contrary, with the preconceived idea of statehood, to which they
then pretend to accommodate the reality of the people. The "51st
state" is like a garment in a show-window, that does not fit Puerto
Rico and that, moreover, cannot be made to fit. The only way

for this garment to fit Puerto Rico would be for the latter to mutilate its body and personality, a terrible cruelty that defines the spirit of utopia. This spirit has been described as

> the tendency to construct patterns greatly at variance with existing reality and feeling that these patterns ought to be realized regardless of the destruction that their realization may imply, . . . the sharp conflict with the forces of history, the awe-inspiring mutilations that have to be consented to if utopia ever is to assume real existence.[103]

Concerning the utopia of the "51st state," former governor of Puerto Rico, Rafael Hernández Colón, writes:

> The main consequence of the social impact of statehood would be the lack of employment and the consequent freezing of social mobility more or less as it was in the 30's: a few rich, a few professionals, and huge, exploited mass of former farmers, former businessmen, and former government officials, joining what Michael Harrington called "the people who stayed behind," in a type of massive ghetto, standing in line to receive federal aid.
>
> The massification [*masificación*] of the middle class entails, morally and psychologically, a predisposition to surrender to any near or distant power that may offer security. In these cases dependency becomes a philosophy of life. Freedom, autonomy, self-respect, social and national identity become illusions of the imagination. Nostalgia and probably deep resentment destroy creative action and self-realization in one's own community, profession or institution. Such an automatization [*automización*] of social and national ties

through economic crises and dependency on dis-
tant powers annihilate both personal initiative and
national identity.[104]

For the statehood movement, political status is not a means
to serve the people, rather the people are the means to serve the
"51ˢᵗ state"; "statehood," not the happiness of the people, is the
end for the sake of which the people are sacrificed.

According to Muñoz, the tenacious insistence of statehooders
and *independentistas* on patently false and destructive alternatives suggests strong irrational elements in their positions. In fact,
upon examining their arguments, Muñoz found wishful thinking, half-truths, and manifest lies. We have mentioned that
statehooders, for example, tried to explain away the disastrous
effects of their status formula on the island's economy by draw-
ing on a supposed increase in federal aid under statehood. Muñoz
claimed that no such input would compensate for the destruction of the economy and that, supposing that to some degree it
did, it would entail the conversion of Puerto Rico into a "beggar
state." The *independentistas*, on the other hand, speculated that
the United States could always give preferential treatment to the
Republic of Puerto Rico.[105] But Muñoz observed that even the
nation enjoying the best treatment by the United States did not
have the free access to the protected American market that Puerto
Rico had as part of the union. Muñoz concluded that the arguments of the annexationists and separatists did not answer to
reality. Their starting point was not in the facts but in a preconceived idea (statehood or independence), in justification of which
they went out looking for facts, or made the facts fit the theory..
Muñoz called this kind of logic "rationalization."[106] This way of
thinking corresponds to what Simon calls an "ideology," namely,
a doctrine or body of statements that imitates philosophy but
that is really an attempt to validate emotional aspirations that do
not necessarily coincide with truth:

According to the familiar use of the word, an ideology is a system of propositions which, though
undistinguishable so far as expression goes from
statements about facts and essences, actually refer
not so much to any real state of affairs as to the
aspirations of a *society* at a certain *time* in its evolution. . . . When what is actually an expression of
aspirations assumes the form of statements about
things, when these aspirations are those of a defi-
nite group, and when that group expresses its
timely aspirations in the language of everlasting
truth—then, without a doubt, it is an ideology
that we are dealing with. . . .

Ideological propositions are not necessarily
deceitful, although any truth entrusted to an ideology is exposed to all sorts of dangers. . . .

The object of an ideology is, in spite of ap-
pearances without which the ideology would not
work, an object of desire. The object of philosophy is a pure object.[107]

Doctrines such as that there are two and only two possible
solutions to the political status question, or that "independence"
and "freedom" are identical, or that there is one and only one
dignified way of joining the American union, for example, are
clearly "ideological" in the sense described. What they affirm as
truths are really dogmatic prejudices offered by the extremists as
"reasons" to attack the Commonwealth and advance their own
cause.

In a speech delivered in Barranquitas on 17 July 1963, Muñoz
refutes other fallacies of annexationist "ideology." Historically
the people have been made to believe that (1) the Commonwealth is not sovereign, (2) that the Commonwealth is basically
a colony, (3) that American citizenship under the Commonwealth
is a "second class" citizenship, (4) that the enhancement of the

Commonwealth entails the loss of American citizenship, (5) that the defenders of the Commonwealth are really promoting independence for Puerto Rico in a disguised way, (6) that, since the states are prosperous, therefore, if Puerto Rico should become a state, it would also be prosperous. To the contention that Puerto Rico is not sovereign, Muñoz answered that sovereignty, as the authority of a people over its own government, takes many forms: a state, a republic, and the Commonwealth are all sovereign in different ways. Besides, in contrast with the utopianism of his opponents, Muñoz held that

> Sovereignty is not a document saying that there is sovereignty. Sovereignty is a bond of forces that produces the real power to execute to a certain extent—never absolutely—the will of a people.[108]

During the Cold War, statehooders (and *independentistas*) joined Fidel Castro and Communist propaganda in labeling the Commonwealth as "a colony, but with perfume sprinkled over it" claims that Muñoz considered not only demagogic, but also an insult to Puerto Rico and the United States. To the annexationist leaders' contention that American citizenship under Commonwealth is a second class citizenship, Muñoz retorted that there is only one American citizenship, so that there is no such thing as "second class American citizenship." To the claim that the culmination of the Commonwealth entails the loss of American citizenship, Muñoz replied that, if American citizenship cannot be taken away from any one individual except in extraordinary circumstances in a court of law, it is less likely that it can be taken away from a whole community. To the accusation that the defenders of the Commonwealth are really promoting independence for Puerto Rico in a disguised way, Muñoz retorted that the Commonwealth means permanent union with the United States and that, had he been a separatist, left wing terrorists would not have repeatedly tried to assassinate him. To the argument, which is sophistry, that since the states are prosperous, therefore, if Puerto Rico should become a state, it would also be prosperous—a fallacy known as *non causa pro causa*—Muñoz replied that states are prosperous not on account of their being states, but because they are rich in resources; so rich, in fact, that they can prosper *in spite* of being states and having to sustain two governments, the local and the federal one, since they are subject to the uniform application of the taxation laws of the United States. In his speech Muñoz concluded that the history of the annexationist parties is brimming with "intellectual dishonesty."

Muñoz was convinced that the people of Puerto Rico would never support such abstract ideologies and that Congress, for its part, would never admit a "beggar state" into the Union. Hence Muñoz always thought of independence and statehood as impossible in practice, at least in the foreseeable future. Since the insistence on changing from Commonwealth to some other status presupposed that statehood and independence were feasible alternatives, and since, for Muñoz, this was not the case, therefore, the whole controversy about political status was for him a sterile and pernicious discussion, a "tema fantasma" or ghost issue.[109] To say that statehood or independence was just around the corner (e.g., "statehood now"), or that "someday" they would come, was for Muñoz a "myth" in the Simonian sense of a false prediction, that gives way to a malign collective enthusiasm:

> A myth imitates the prediction of a fact, and by filling the minds and hearts of men with a certain anticipation it exerts an influence on the course of history, even though actual developments may be widely at variance with the fact anticipated.[110]
>
> * * *
>
> Myths are not descriptions of things, but expressions of determination to act.[111]
>
> * * *
>
> Now, between the most vicious and the most vir-

tuous forms of collective enthusiasm there are psychological and sociological analogies which render opportune the employment of a common term. That of *mystique*, launched by Péguy on a celebrated page (Charles Péguy, *Notre jeunesse* [Paris: Gallimard, 1910]: 26), would not be bad. We propose, then, to call heroic faiths those *mystiques* in which truth and justice predominate, and to reserve the name of *myths* for those in which error and evil predominate.[112]

Muñoz observed that the persistence of annexationist and separatist leaders in pursuinG their "myths" has often included demagogy and violence.[113] Holding on to their extreme ideas on status with the blindness of fanatics, they have wanted to impose their formulas on the people. Among the moral flaws which, according to Muñoz, did not let them appreciate the issue of political status as "uniquely determined," he included what he considered one of the worst enemies of the modern world, corrosive of the human spirit and threatening to the survival of mankind: the sentiment of nationalism. According to Muñoz, many *independentistas* wanted separation from the United States simply because they were nationalists who strove after a pure and sacrosanct culture, closed within itself, suspicious of others.[114] At the same time, Muñoz held that if you scratch the surface of many statehooders there is a nationalist underneath, only the nationality they idolize is not Puerto Rican, but American. Indeed, in "El status político de Puerto Rico," his speech delivered on 3 June 1959, Muñoz accused assimilationist leaders of intentionally or unconsciously deprecating everything autochthonous and of trying to make Puerto Ricans feel inferior by suggesting that theyt are worthy only because the American flag waves over the island. This attitude, he remarked, compares with that of inconditional supporters of the Spanish under Spanish dominion, who thought that only the Spaniards and things Spanish

were worthwhile, and that the Puerto Ricans were no good.[115]
Against this position of the statehooders, Muñoz commented
that he could not conceive how someone could consider himself
to be a good American citizen if he was ashamed of his own
origins.

It is easier to understand the political imprudence of insist-
ing—in Muñoz's time—on independence for Puerto Rico, and
such an aberration as the Puerto Rican assimilationist movement,
if, following Muñoz, one thinks of the "republic" and the "51st
state" as *utopias* supported by *ideologies* and proclaimed as *myths*.

NOTES

92. See Chapters 1 and 2.

93. Muñoz Marín, "Breakthrough from Nationalism," Lecture II.

94. Muñoz Marín, Speech delivered in Maricao on 17 September 1952.

95. Muñoz Marín, *Discursos*, 117-18, 136-37, 380; Yves R. Simon, *Philosophy of Democratic Government* (Chicago: The University of Chicago Press, 1951), 29.

96. Muñoz Marín, Speech delivered at the *Asociación de Alcaldes* in San Juan on 1959. My translation.

97. Ibid.

98. Yves R. Simon, *The Community of the Free*, trans. Willard R. Task (New York: Holt & Co., 1947), 167-68; *Philosophy of Democratic Government*, 91, 128-43.

99. Muñoz Marín, "Development Through Democracy," 1.

100. Ibid., 2.

101. Muñoz Marín, "El status político de Puerto Rico," Speech delivered on 4 June 1959. My translation.

102. Muñoz Marín, Speech delivered at the Lions Club of San Juan on 22 July 1959.

103. Simon, *Philosophy of Democratic Government*, 91, 128-43.

104. Rafael Hernández Colón, *Retos y luchas* (San Juan: Rafael Hernández Colón, 1991), 146.

105. Muñoz Marín, Speech delivered in Barranquitas on 17 July 1951; *Discursos*, 290-91.

106. Muñoz Marín, Speech delivered at the *Asociación de Alcaldes* on 1959. See also "El status político de Puerto Rico," Speech delivered on 4 June 1959; *Discursos*, 285-86.

107. Yves R. Simon, *The Tradition of Natural Law*, ed. Vukan Kuic, with a foreword by John H. Hallowell (New York: Fordham University Press, 1965), 16-21.

108. Muñoz Marín, *Memorias: autobiografía pública [1940-1952]*, 170. My translation. Muñoz clearly subscribed to what is known as "the transmission theory of sovereignty." According to this view, God is the absolute sovereign and source of all power, who expresses his authority through the natural law of all nations. Through these laws God gives a subordinated sovereignty to the people, to the community as a whole; in other words, he gives them the natural right to govern themselves. The people may in turn retain that sovereignty for themselves—and then a system of direct democracy ensues—or they may *transmit* their sovereignty to some specific agency or distinct personnel by whom they consent to be governed. In this case the people designate a person or assembly as their ruler and then transmit their God-given sovereignty to them.

109. Luis Muñoz Marín, "El status político de Puerto Rico," Speech delivered on 3 June 1959.

110. Simon, *The Tradition of Natural Law*, 21.

111. Georges Sorel, *Reflections on Violence*, trans. T. E. Hulme (New York: Viking Press, 1914), 32, quoted in Simon, *The Tradition of Natural Law*, 173.

112. Yves R. Simon, *The March to Liberation*, trans. Victor M. Hamm (Milwaukee: The Tower Press, 1942), 23.

113. Muñoz Marín, Speech delivered in Barranquitas on 17 July 1963; *Discursos*, 167-72, 450-51.

114. Muñoz Marín, *Discursos*, 211, 268, 470.

115. Muñoz Marín, Speech delivered at the *Asociación de Alcaldes* on 1959; *Discursos*, 454-55.

CHAPTER 5

THE NATURE AND VALUES OF
THE COMMONWEALTH

The Nature of the Commonwealth

According to Muñoz, the very people of Puerto Rico decided to create their own political truth instead of merely copying formulas that have worked well for other communities in markedly different circumstances. In cooperation with Congress the Puerto Ricans designed a new form of liberty that expedited, instead of obstructing, their development of a good civilization.

Puerto Rico, as a personal community, has temporal and supratemporal tendencies and needs. According to Thomistic philosophy,[116] the first of these tendencies is to remain in existence, to preserve its identity, which is a tendency and teleology that it shares with all entities as such. At the biological and the psychological levels, Puerto Rico represents a distinct ethnic group with African, Spanish, Taíno, and Latin American roots. It has characteristic forms of being, and thus enjoys autonomy even in questions of psycho-physical individuality. With its spirituality, rationality and freedom of choice, Puerto Rico manifests itself as a creator of culture. By nature it embodies a sovereign community with the right to exercise authority over itself, and the vocation to govern itself and choose its own form of government. Like all persons, whether individual or collective, it possesses a social nature which requires the cultivation of friends from whom to receive and to whom to give disinterestedly. Here is the tendency to seek complementary relations by joining a wider whole, a comprehensive common good in genuine communion. Union serves not only to meet needs as lacks, but also to widen horizons through spiritual and cultural expansion.

All these traits, which enter into the make-up of Puerto Rico, involve laws that must be respected if this community is to attain its true good and develop according to its natural and authentic modes of being. If the Thomists are right, to achieve the higher autonomy of the person, which is ultimate freedom of choice, virtue and self-government, Puerto Rico must internalize these laws related to its true good and choose the right means that will lead to its given end.[117] It was this kind of autonomy that Muñoz had in mind with the establishment of the Commonwealth. The Commonwealth was custom-made for Puerto Rico, it was designed with integral liberty and the good of the people of Puerto Rico in mind.

In "El status político de Puerto Rico," a speech delivered on 4 June 1959, as well as in the Godkin Lectures, Muñoz explains that the procedure for establishing the Commonwealth was identical to the one followed when a new state is admitted to the union. The people of Puerto Rico, through their legitimate representatives, expressed their desire to become a state of a new kind and to be thus permanently united with the United States. Congress approved the corresponding "enabling act," Public Law 600, on the basis of which a Puerto Rican Constitutional convention drafted a constitution which was submitted to the electorate and approved by popular vote, and which was later submitted to and approved by Congress. Public Law 600 expressly states that the principle of government by consent was thereby "fully recognized,"[118] and that the Act was adopted "in the nature of a compact,"[119] which means that it cannot be revoked unilaterally by either of the parties. Some specific sections of the Jones Act, the organic law then in effect, referring mostly to international issues, were deemed to have been repealed, while others, dealing largely with the terms of the relationship between the United States and Puerto Rico, remained in force and were known as the Puerto Rico Federal Relations Act. This act contains, among other things, the provisions concerning one of the pillars of the Puerto Rico-United States relationship: common citizenship. Common citizenship implies: that federal laws, except the tax laws, would apply to the American citizens of Puerto Rico; that these citizens would have the right to juridical appeal to the federal courts; and that a federal court would be established in Puerto Rico. The Federal Relations Act also guaranteed free trade between the United States and Puerto Rico, as well as common coinage, a customs union, and the seating of a Resident Commissioner of Puerto Rico in Washington. Public Law 600 was overwhelmingly accepted by the people of Puerto Rico, the Constitution was drafted and adopted, and the Commonwealth which it created, under a political status known as "association by compact"[120] and recognized by the United Nations as a kind of "free association," was formally established on 25 July 1952.

Under the Commonwealth relationship, Puerto Rico is obviously neither an independent republic nor a federated state; it is not a possession, territory or any kind of colony of the United States: "It is a new kind of state, *both* in the sense of the U. S. Federal System and in the general sense of a people organized to govern themselves."[121] As a Commonwealth, Puerto Rico became an autonomous body politic in association with the United States. It became at once a non-federated (associated) state and a non-independent (associated) country. Like a superior synthesis, the Commonwealth embodies the best part of statehood and the best part of independence, while avoiding their respective pitfalls for the island. According to Muñoz, the Commonwealth represents statehood without assimilationism, independence without separatism, and nationality without nationalism:

> In essence the status of Puerto Rico is: either that
> of an independent republic, with common citi-

zenship with the United States, having its foreign policy, like the other political communities composed of citizens of the United States, through the government of the American union, enjoying free trade with the United States, having its own constitutional government; or that of a state of the union, without contributing taxes to the federal Treasury, therefore without voting representation in the federal Congress.[122]

In his speech delivered at the Lions Club of San Juan on 22 July 1959, as well as in his *Discursos,* Muñoz explains that, as a Commonwealth, Puerto Rico enjoys the same dignity that a state does even though it varies in form. Exactly like a state, Puerto Rico governs itself through its own constitution, which it can amend; it elects its own legislature and governor and establishes a judiciary which includes the Supreme Court of Puerto Rico, from which appeals can be made to the Supreme Court of the United States. In contrast with a federated state, however, Puerto Rico has no senators or representatives in Congress; it only has a Resident Commissioner with no vote. Following the principle of "no taxation without representation," Puerto Rico does not pay one cent of all the federal taxes that states must uniformly pay. Since the compact that joins Puerto Rico to the Union is Law 600 and not the American Constitution per se, this union, though permanent by its very nature (e.g., through the bond of citizenship), is more flexible than that of the states, which have sealed their destinies once and for all, and whose relations to the Union are harder to modify. In sum, the federated state and the associated state, though equal in dignity, differ in that the latter enjoys much more overall autonomy than the former.

Due to this greater autonomy, Puerto Rico has also the dignity of an independent country; for example, it has an international dimension that no state can have. Like an independent country, Puerto Rico drafted its own constitution, elects its own legislature and executive, and establishes its own judiciary, including a supreme court. While in an independent nation appeals would end in its Supreme court, Puerto Ricans can, under Commonwealth, also reach the Supreme Court of the United States. In an independent country no American federal laws apply, but in Puerto Rico most do, except for the tax laws. Muñoz pointed out that, if Puerto Rico were an independent country, it would always seek treatment as "most favored nation"[123] in the market of the United States, so as to pay as little as possible in tariffs. But the amount the island actually pays in tariffs under the free trade disposition of the Commonwealth is optimal, namely, zero.

Muñoz saw Commonwealth status, not just as a new status formula, but as a vital political creation with ample space for growth. To illustrate this creative relationship between Puerto Rico and the United States, Muñoz compared it with a Martini. In a speech delivered at a Press Club Luncheon in Washington, D. C., on 6 May 1952, Muñoz says that Puerto Rico cannot be the gin in a Martini, because a Martini takes too much gin. Neither can the island play the role of the vermouth for the same reason. Puerto Rico can be either the drop of angostura or the olive. Now if it were the drop of angostura, it would be dissolved and lost. But as the olive, Muñoz concludes, Puerto Rico gives a touch of distinction to the drink, making it worthy to be served in the Western Hemisphere.

The Commonwealth and the Good for Puerto Rico

The advantages of Commonwealth status are varied and many, both material and spiritual, and benefit Puerto Rico as well as the United States, Latin America and the rest of the world. Moreover, these advantages are not hypothetical but have actually been verified. Statehood and independence being quixotic for cultural and socio-economic reasons, the Commonwealth arose as the only instrument capable of guaranteeing economic as well as genuine (not merely formal) political liberty, and thus of obtaining for Puerto Rico the conditions of the cultural ideal of the good life.

Through the Commonwealth, Puerto Rico left extreme poverty behind to become one of the most progressive countries in the world, second only to Japan in its rate of economic growth. American and other companies, thanks to the tax exemption that Puerto Rico could offer them by virtue of its fiscal autonomy, invested their capital in Puerto Rico, making rapid industrialization possible. These companies also accounted for a great number of direct and indirect jobs in Puerto Rico. Free trade with the United States and the extension of federal programs to the island constituted other vital assets that the Commonwealth could use for the economic ideal of Puerto Rico.

In addition to the economic ideal, Commonwealth also achieved the political ideal for Puerto Rico as regards both the question of political status and the practice of democracy. Since even before the Commonwealth relationship was in effect, Puerto Ricans could elect their own government officials, Muñoz thought that, in fact, Puerto Rico had stopped being a colony long before the establishment of the Commonwealth.[124] The only disadvantage, he said, was that the written law did not reflect this. But, according to Muñoz, once Puerto Rico drafted its own constitution under Law 600, its relationship with the United States ceased to be based on military occupation, or on the Treaty of Paris, or on the plenary powers of Congress under the Territorial Clause of the Constitution, and the relationship was thereafter founded on the compact established by Law 600. Muñoz claimed that with this compact the law was brought up to date with the freedom which was already a fact of life on the island. In his speech at the Press Club luncheon of 6 May 1952, he compared this event to the situation of a man who owns a house but who has not yet got the deed to the house; upon receiving title of ownership, something significant happens even though the house has always been his: "The idea of a 'compact' makes a basic change in the relationship. It takes away from the very basis of the prior relationship—the nature and onus of colonialism."[125]

According to Muñoz, the free agreement on which the Commonwealth is based is the decisive step in self-government: "Nothing can be freer than a free agreement . . . There can be no greater political dignity than that of a free agreement—because a free super-agreement or a super-free agreement are inconceivable."[126] Commonwealth thus represents a new way of abolishing colonial status under the constitutional system of the United States. Through this status, the relationship between the United States and Puerto Rico stopped resembling that between "a good master and an affectionate servant,"[127] and it thus acquired a "deeply respectable moral basis."[128] After this agreement was reached, the United States stopped sending information about the territory of Puerto Rico to the United Nations under Article 73e of the Charter. As Congresswoman Frances P. Bolton explained:

> The relationships previously established . . . by a law of Congress, which only Congress can amend, have now become provisions of a compact of a bilateral nature whose terms may be changed only by consent.[129]

Muñoz thought that the Commonwealth, besides solving the issue of political status by ending the legal traces of despotism, also fulfils the political ideal by optimizing the actual practice of democracy. We have seen that what distinguishes democracy as a superior form of government is the fact that it goes beyond preserving autonomy to *maximizing* it.[130] In this sense Commonwealth constitutes a superb example of the practice of democracy, because it maximizes the power of the votes of the Puerto Ricans, who are empowered to attack the problems that directly affect them and to take care of their own affairs and destiny within the pursuit of the common good.

Commonwealth also provides the opportunity for the spiritual and cultural enhancement implied in forming part of a wider whole in genuine communion. Muñoz recognized that part of the uniqueness of the Puerto Rican people is its non-isolationist and non-nationalistic personality. In his address delivered on the occasion of the fifth anniversary of the Commonwealth's founding, on 25 July 1957, he said that Puerto Ricans, as creators of culture, should not remain static or closed within themselves, because culture is something dynamic that must be open to change, so long as that change is authentic and responds to the people's own ways of experiencing life. According to Muñoz, one of the greatest values of Commonwealth is precisely that it does justice to this non-nationalist, non-isolationist character of the people of Puerto Rico. The significance of this feature of the Commonwealth, in the eyes of Muñoz, lies in the world's urgent need to tame the "wild horses"[131] of nationalism, a monster that, as Muñoz warned, threatens to destroy not one nation or another, but humanity itself through the power of nuclear weapons. Muñoz claimed that the people of Puerto Rico, as is reflected in their political status, have bypassed and transcended nationalism. He thought that this breakthrough achieved by a small Latin American island anticipates a necessary attitude in the world and involves a new way of conceiving of a nation, a people, a political society:

> Here is a society that believes in freedom more than in sovereignty [in the presumptuous sense], that believes in having a healthy pride in itself, a sense of itself and of its cultural personality, yet feels loyally at ease in the context of its close association with that vast power that Latin America long referred to as the Colossus of the North.[132]

The Commonwealth achieves the good for the particular community of Puerto Rico, because it represents far more political autonomy, more power through the ballot box for its citizens than could have been achieved through statehood or independence. It achieves genuine decolonization through the establishment of a democratic compact, even while securing economic freedom. Furthermore, the Commonwealth allows Puerto Ricans to develop their own ways of life, to be more in control of the kind of civilization their spirit would wish to develop. In short, the Commonwealth achieves the economic, political, and cultural ideals of Puerto Rico, and this in the face of the fact that there was no other means to achieve them.

The Commonwealth and the Good for the United States, Latin America and the World

To the extent that Puerto Rico, as part of the United States, achieves its ends and is not overwhelmed by the whole, in that same measure the whole (the United States) gains in plenitude. The Commonwealth, in realizing the true good for Puerto Rico, enhances the American union and contributes to it. For Muñoz, one of the most important contributions Puerto Rico makes to the union is to promote its diversity.[133] Muñoz thought that one of the greatest values of American citizenship is its recognition of the right of individuals and groups to differ and to develop spontaneously. For him diversity was a natural outgrowth and a sign of freedom: freedom allows for diversity, even while diversity preserves freedom. Muñoz understood that all citizens of the United States should agree in regard to certain attitudes such as loyalty to the values and the defense of democracy. But he thought that, beyond uniform adherence to such common values, there is a right and even a duty to preserve diversity for the sake of individual well-being and the plenitude of the whole:

> Diversity within unity. It is to that image of creative diversity within the equally creative great whole, . . . to that realization, that flowering and enrichment, that Puerto Rico wants to contribute in its association with the United States.[134]

Commonwealth, based on "the political and human principle that uniformity becomes justified only when it is necessary for a higher end,"[135] achieves the enhancement of the whole of the United States of America (which, Muñoz said, thus also becomes the "United *Peoples* of America"[136]) through a deepening of the principle of "E Pluribus Unum."

Commonwealth achieves equality without creating sterile similarity. Muñoz believed that adding a new state to the Union does not contribute any richness of cultural or political content to it. On the other hand, he thought that establishing an association in equally dignified but distinct terms adapted to the circumstances of Puerto Rico was of great service and enhancement to the union. Muñoz argued, for example, that while good relations between a state and the union do not carry any particularly special message to the world, the relationship of the Commonwealth of Puerto Rico with the United States does carry a message to Latin America and the rest of the world, including those areas where anti-American propaganda abounds. It is the message of "the understanding between two cultures under a single citizenship in voluntary association, based on sincere affection, clear understanding and good will."[137] But if Puerto Rico were homogenized, as was attempted at the beginning of the colonization, this value would be lost, thought Muñoz. If the part were to lose its identity or personality, not only would it suffer loss of life, but so the broader communities of which it forms part would be impoverished.

According to Muñoz, Puerto Rico is "culturally a Latin American country, composed of good citizens of the United States."[138] In this sense it is a kind of "political mutation"[139] in the Americas, a fact which, for Muñoz, accounted for its special usefulness as "cultural frontier and passageway of understanding and good will between the Americas."[140] Muñoz believed that precisely because of its uniqueness the island can contribute to a better understanding of the United States in Latin America and the rest of the world. For example, Puerto Rico has surpassed economic misery with political creativity and the help of the United States. Now upon observing the amazing progress of Puerto Rico, the world sees that this is done with the encouragement and support of the United States, "with no strings attached, save the strings of mutual trust and respect."[141] For Muñoz, Puerto Rico's importance as a military base of the United States in the Caribbean is overshadowed by its importance as a "civic base"[142] and symbol of democracy. He thought that the "enlightened relationship"[143] of the Commonwealth is a credit to the United States throughout the world and furnishes a refutation of the accusations of imperialism that have been levelled against it. Muñoz claimed that the Commonwealth of Puerto Rico

> . . . is the acid test of United States attitudes regarding colonialism and economic imperialism, and the whole big problem of how to deal with a people from a different culture, emerging out of an agrarian economy. This is a showcase for the intentions of the United States.[144]

Muñoz argued that Puerto Rico contributes to the policies and prestige of the United States as the latter faces the responsibility of championing the cause of freedom, peace and democracy in the world. The Commonwealth, Muñoz thought, is "a lesson on the good will deserved by the United States of America in its difficult task of defending democracy, helping to raise standards of living in the world, and ensuring peace."[145] Muñoz believed that the challenge to freedom would ultimately take the form of an ideological clash between the attempt to defeat economic poverty by political slavery and the purpose of enhancing political and human freedom through economic productivity and social justice. He held that the answer to the Communist challenge lay in the ability of the Western powers, and especially of the United States, to show the poor countries of the world that a greater transformation can be achieved, at an even faster rate and on sounder economic foundations, "without shattering, or ignoring, as the Russians and the Red Chinese have done, the fabric of political and individual liberties."[146]

On the other hand, Muñoz thought that the United States should treat Latin American countries in the same way that it has treated Puerto Rico, namely, as fellow-citizens.[147] He thought that the United States should help Latin America in achieving the changes demanded by justice and democracy, without requiring that those changes coincide with American viewpoints, so long as they sprang out of the peoples concerned, and provided that the principles of respect towards the individual and of government through the consent of the governed are safeguarded. For example, Muñoz thought that the United States should not identify liberty with capitalism, or condemn alternate means to achieve economic justice, so long as those means respected individual rights and guarantees. He also pointed out that the United States should carefully distinguish between those anti-Communist Latin American leaders who are also anti-democratic and those who are truly democratic.

Puerto Rico, thanks to its unique experience, has made significant contributions to the underdeveloped countries which seek economic and political liberation but cannot find the solution to their problems in traditional status formulas or old forms of federation. Muñoz never suggested that other communities should merely imitate Puerto Rico. On the contrary, in his speech on 5 July 1952, he claimed that what Puerto Rico had to offer was precisely the proof that countries in extremely difficult circumstances need neither descend to degradation nor commit suicide, but that, if they seek their wisdom within, they can create their own solutions to their own problems.[148] He insisted, for example, that new forms are necessary to equip the world with more options for union, cooperation, association and federation that could link, on the basis of justice and freedom, the variety of ways of life that has developed and will keep developing through history. Muñoz thought that federalism is the future of the world and that new forms should be contributed to it.[149] He said that the Commonwealth of Puerto Rico represents a new form of political freedom in federal association. While the states that joined the original thirteen American colonies merely imitated the political creation of the latter, Puerto Rico developed a whole new form of permanent union and hence a new form of political liberty. Like the original thirteen colonies, Puerto Rico is a "pioneer."[150] Puerto Rico adds a new dimension and an original way for both the political principle of federation in general and the American system in particular to develop. The case of Puerto Rico furnishes living proof that a community in unique circumstances could still be part of the American Union and loyal to it without sacrificing economic or political freedom. This new form of state does not hurt the federation in any way but, on the contrary, enhances it, at the same time that it allows more liberty to Puerto Rico. Muñoz used to quote Justice Earl Warren's appraisal of this feat of political creativity:

> In the sense that our American system is not static, in the sense that it is an organism intended to grow and expand to meet varying conditions and times in a large country—in the sense that every governmental effort of ours is an experiment—so the new institutions of the Commonwealth of Puerto Rico represent an experiment—the newest experiment and perhaps the most notable of American governmental experiments in our lifetimes.[151]

In Muñoz's mind the Commonwealth deserves to be recognized, beyond being a contribution to the American political system, as "one of the most significant signs of democratic maturity and political creativity of our century."[152]

The autonomy of Puerto Rico thus achieves ethical, political, and pragmatic values that benefit the smaller society which is part of the whole, as well as the whole as such, including the United States, Latin America, and the world. Muñoz believed, in agreement with Thomistic doctrine, that progress in the autonomy of Puerto Rico is equivalent to the spiritual expansion, growth in virtue and genuine emancipation of Puerto Ricans. Puerto Rico's autonomy adds prestige to the United States by showing how the latter has dealt with a smaller country of a different culture without overwhelming it but, quite the contrary, by being a genuine friend and offering a helping hand in the economic and political liberation of the island. And to the extent that Puerto Rico's autonomy becomes enhanced, in that same measure it brings prestige to the United States.[153] Furthermore, insofar as Puerto Rico has the ability to deal with its own problems in its own ways, efficiency is achieved within the United States. The strengthening of Puerto Rico's economy, for example, besides ending dependency on federal aid, automatically benefits the economy of the United States, in whose market the island participates. As regards the beneficial impact of the Commonwealth on the rest of the world, it must be mentioned that, by developing its own forms of solving its own problems, Puerto Rico sets an example to the underdeveloped countries of the world, exemplifying locally created ways and programs to face extreme poverty and other problems. In addition, Commonwealth means leadership in transcending the narrowness of nationalism in a war-weary world. Today nationalist sentiment accounts for the violence taking place in Northern Ireland, former Yugoslavia, the northern part of Spain, and former Soviet Union, to mention just a few places.

NOTES

116. Simon, *Nature and Functions of Authority*, 43.

117. See Chapter 1.

118. Muñoz Marín, "Breakthrough from Nationalism," Lecture II.

119 Ibid.

120. Muñoz Marín, *Mensajes*, 110. Muñoz distinguished between the *status* of Puerto Rico and the *constitutional creation* devised under that status. The status of Puerto Rico he called "association by compact," while the Commonwealth (*Estado Libre Asociado* in Spanish) is properly the constitutional entity created under that status (*Mensajes*, 110).

121. Luis Muñoz Marín, "An America to Serve the World," Speech delivered on 7 April 1956. Emphasis added.

122. Muñoz Marín, Inaugural address delivered in San Juan on 2 January 1953.

123. Muñoz Marín, Speech delivered in Barranquitas on 17 July 1951. See also *Discursos*, 290-91.

124. Muñoz Marín, *Discursos*, 336-42.

125. Muñoz Marín, "Breakthrough from Nationalism," Lecture II.

126. Muñoz Marín, *Discursos*, 384.

127. Muñoz Marín, "El status político de Puerto Rico," Speech delivered on 4 June 1959.

128. Ibid.

129. Muñoz Marín, "Breakthrough from Nationalism," Lecture II.

130. Simon, *Philosophy of Democratic Government*, 142. 184. See also Chapter 3.

131. Muñoz Marín, "Breakthrough from Nationalism," Lecture I.

132. Muñoz Marín, Address delivered at Bate College on 9 June 1957.

133. Muñoz Marín, "The Deep Significance of United States Citizenship," Address delivered on the occasion of the fourth anniversary of the Commonwealth on 25 July 1956; Address delivered on 4 July 1964.

134. Muñoz Marín, "The Deep Significance of United States Citizenship."

135. Muñoz Marín, "El status político de Puerto Rico," Speech delivered on 4 June 1959.

136. Muñoz Marín, *Discursos*, 277. Emphasis added. My translation.

137. Muñoz Marín, Notes for a speech delivered at the Rotary Club of San Juan on 28 July 1953.

138. Luis Muñoz Marín, "Facts Forum's State of the Nation," Radio program in which Muñoz was interviewed by Harwood Hull in San Juan on 9 March 1954.

139. Ibid.

140. Muñoz Marín, "La personalidad puertorriqueña en el Estado Libre Asociado," Speech given at the *Asamblea General de la Asociación de Maestros de Puerto Rico* on 29 December 1953. My translation.

141. Luis Muñoz Marín, "Puerto Rico's Role in International Cooperation," Address delivered at the Inaugural Session of the ICA Conference of Mission Directors and Program Staff of Latin American Area in San Juan on 27 January 1958.

142. Luis Muñoz Marín, Speech delivered at a Press Club Luncheon in Washington, D.C. on 6 May 1952.

143. Muñoz Marín, Address at Bate College on 9 June 1957.

144. Muñoz Marín, "Puerto Rico's Role in International Cooperation."

145. Muñoz Marín, Speech delivered at the Rotary Club of Santurce on 12 November 1958.

146. Muñoz Marín, "An America to Serve the World," Speech delivered on 7 April 1956.

147. Luis Muñoz Marín, Speech delivered on the occasion of receiving the Liberty Award granted by the Liberty House on 7 October 1956.

148. See also Congress, Committee on Foreign Relations,

Foreign Policy Review: Hearing held before the Committee on Foreign Relations, 10 March 1958; Muñoz Marín, Speech delivered at the Rotary Club of Santurce on 12 November 1958.

149. Muñoz Marín, Speech delivered at the Lions Club of San Juan on 22 July 1959; Speech delivered at the Rotary Club of Santurce on 12 November 1958; Address delivered on 4 July 1964; "El status político de Puerto Rico," Speech delivered on 4 June 1959; *Discursos*, 344.

150. Muñoz Marín, "Puerto Rico Does Not Want to Be a State," 36.

151. Muñoz Marín, "Breakthrough from Nationalism," Lecture II.

152. Muñoz Marín, Address delivered on 4 July 1964.

153. Inversely, to the extent that the autonomy of Puerto Rico appears stagnant or scant, in that same measure does the deep sense of the association become weakened and the United States risks being labeled as "imperialist."

CHAPTER 6

THE DEVELOPMENT OF COMMONWEALTH AND THE PRINCIPLE OF AUTONOMY

Though the Commonwealth achieved the ideals of the people of Puerto Rico, Muñoz admitted that it was not perfect, just as nothing human is perfect. Besides, he always argued that the Commonwealth should be viewed not as a static formula, but rather as a vital and dynamic creation with ample scope for growth. Yet Muñoz stressed that the development of Commonwealth was not a stepping stone to statehood or independence or any other status. For him the Commonwealth is not a transitional status but a political end in itself: "it is not a cocoon awaiting the emergence of a butterfly. It is a young butterfly of a new species, and it is still growing."[154] While theoretically Commonwealth left the doors open to statehood or independence, it is, according to Muñoz, permanent by its very nature and can and should grow according to that nature. It was precisely in this growth that Muñoz saw the strengthening and consolidation of the Commonwealth.

One imperfection which Muñoz found in Commonwealth is that the kind of consent given to the non-tax federal laws was generic. Consenting to these federal laws as a block results, he believed, in an imperfect form of participation, inasmuch as some laws from the old Organic Act were consented to that really should not apply to the Commonwealth. Hence Muñoz saw the natural development of Commonwealth mainly as a perfecting of the participation of the Puerto Ricans in the federal sphere through "trying to convert the generic form of consent to the non-tax federal legislation into a specific consent to specific laws."[155] This means that fewer kinds of federal laws would apply on the basis of the original generic consent and that more kinds would apply only through the specific consent of the people of Puerto Rico as expressed through their democratically elected authorities. Forms of participation compatible with the Commonwealth concept (e.g., government to government) would give the people of Puerto Rico a say on the federal decisions, functions and legislation that concern them. For Muñoz this increased participation in federal legislation represents more power for the votes of the Puerto Ricans on election day, more control over matters that directly affect them, and hence a deepening of democracy.

To the extent that federal laws apply that are unnecessary for Puerto Rico, or not essential to the association or to the national interest of the United States as a whole, there was an element of what Simon calls false paternal or substitutional authority.[156] It is false and to that extent oppressive, because *genuine* paternal authority applies only in circumstances of deficiency that make the subject unable to govern himself, and even then it aims at its own disappearance upon the subject's recovery of self-leadership. According to Muñoz, the presence of any trace or even suspicion of paternalism impairs the deep, full significance of the association. He thought that the association should be juridically and morally clarified and freed from all suspicion of paternalism, so as to silence all accusations by Communists and other adversaries of Puerto Rico and the United States, as well as the well-intentioned criticism made by American and Latin American scholars, to the effect that the United States maintains a colonial regime in Puerto Rico.[157]

Surely, if human associations serve the Good for man, they cannot violate his fundamental rights. According to Simon, if the political community is to be truly genuine or just, far from impairing the autonomy of man, it must (1) preserve initial autonomy and (2) promote the evolution of initial into ultimate autonomy.[158] Now the preservation and promotion of autonomy implies, for example, that those functions that can be fulfilled with equal efficiency by either the federation, commonwealth, or state, or by subsidiary groups within the federation, commonwealth, or state, be always assigned to the subsidiary group for the sake of decentralization of power and the development of autonomy. What can be done well by the smaller social unit should never be taken over by the larger one. Thus Simon formulates his "principle of autonomy":

> Wherever a task can be satisfactorily achieved by the initiative of the individual or that of small social units, the fulfillment of that task *must* be left to the initiative of the individual or to that of small social units.[159]

Maritain's analogous "pluralist principle" reads:

> Everything in the body politic which can be brought about by particular organs or societies inferior in degree to the State and born out of the free initiative of the people *should* be brought about by those particular organs or societies.[160]

The principle of autonomy is the foundation of Muñoz's "democratic principle"[161] which is, reciprocally, the application of the principle of autonomy to the particular case of Puerto Rico:

> All that restricts the authority of Puerto Rico in

> Puerto Rico without any appreciable advantage
> to Union and without being essential to the prin-
> ciple of association through common citizenship,
> should be removed from the compact in some
> proper manner at some proper time.[162]

The enhancement of autonomy, which amounts to spiritual growth through the internalization of the law of the good, results in the genuine emancipation of mankind, for ultimate autonomy prevents the enslavement of man—to matter, evil, or his fellow man.[163] For this purpose, authority or government must always be supplemented and balanced by the principle of autonomy:

> The progress of society and freedom requires that
> at every given moment in the evolution of a com-
> munity the greatest possible number of tasks
> should be directly managed by individuals and
> smaller units, the smallest number possible by the
> greater units.[164]

Therefore, if there is an end or function that can be satisfactorily covered by the initiative of an individual or a subsidiary group, but instead is arbitrarily assumed by the larger social unit, the principle of autonomy is violated and we have "a misconception, a perversion of the common good."[165]

A whole that stifles the initiative and, with it, the uniqueness of its parts, becomes impoverished in many ways. Simon discloses this truth through the following example which appears in his article "Common Good and Common Action" and in his book *Philosophy of Democratic Government*. Imagine, he says, a vast plain all of whose parts are homogeneous in that they produce the same crops. Under these conditions farming in the region may be done in two ways. The Department of Agriculture may send diverse teams in charge of the distinct functions of plowing, fertilizing, sowing, etc., and the farming would then be a public affair under the supervision of a branch of government that organizes the division of labor according to the various relevant functions. Or the land may be entrusted to many farmers who own and exercise sovereignty over a distinct part of it. In this case, instead of public land cultivated by "mere instruments of a central agency,"[166] we would then have a "multitude of self-ruling agents."[167]

Simon finds that the latter method is superior to the former in many respects. To begin with, it secures greater pragmatic efficiency. When the land is divided into homesteads, each farmer knows exactly the part entrusted to him, becomes responsible for it, and identifies himself with its care. This method achieves greater order and better quality in production, inasmuch as each farmer concentrates on his property, trying to improve it every day. To the extent that each farmer focuses on his own homestead and goes about his task with dedication and zeal, efficiency grows.

But Simon offers another argument, based on an altogether different consideration than pragmatic efficiency, in favor of the second method. Assuming that both methods of farming are equally efficient and yield the same quantity and quality of production, Simon asks which would be the *better* way to do the job. Here a criterion different from order or efficiency comes into play. All things equal as regards efficiency, Simon concludes that the choice would be between life and lifelessness, between plenitude and emptiness: "Clearly, a whole is better off if its parts are full of initiative than if they are merely traversed by an energy which never becomes their own."[168] In other words, since there is more perfection in life than in death, and since freedom as an absolute perfection is "the glory of the rational nature," the better arrangement would be to let the land be tilled by the many autonomous farmers, instead of placing it in the hands of a single power that absorbs the whole region. Vitality being superior to what is mechanical, a state of affairs brought about vitally is preferable to one obtained mechanically. "It may even be argued," says Simon, "that lesser results obtained through vital processes are more valuable than greater results obtained by curbing the forces of life."[169] Conversely, obtaining an effect through external, mechanical authority, even when it is in harmony with nature, "involves a sort of violence."[170]

Both metaphysically and ethically speaking, plurality is the condition of meaning and plenitude: "A totality which does not admit of autonomous parts disappears into the vacuum caused by its imperialistic arrogance."[171] The more autonomous and unique each part is, the richer and the more perfect the whole becomes. This metaphysical law which establishes that the good of the whole implies the good of its parts, and that a whole is richer the more diverse and specialized are its parts, is the same law which demands that no tasks be assumed by the larger unit of society that can be satisfactorily handled by a smaller unit.[172] Clearly, then, the principle of political autonomy is not a mere policy, but a metaphysical or natural law. Its essence was expressed by Pope Leo XIII in *Rerum Novarum*, where he says that the state should not thrust itself into the peculiar concerns and the organization of the smaller subsidiary societies, "for things move and live by the spirit inspiring them, and may be killed by the rough grasp of a hand from without."[173] For Simon this aspect of the natural law is not obscure, but appears evident to the human understanding:

> It is perfectly obvious that there is more life and, unqualifiedly, greater perfection in a community all parts of which are full of initiative than in a community whose parts act merely as instruments transmitting the initiative of the whole.[174]

Abundance of life and fulness of rational initiative—excellences secured through autonomy—in all parts of the community are paramount aspects of the common good. The tragedy witnessed in totalitarian regimes is precisely that the economic, political, and cultural autonomy of the citizens and of subsidiary communities and institutions is absorbed by a crushing centralization of political power. Václav Havel, president of the Czech Republic, has written that "the greatest enemy of communism always was individuality, variety, difference—in a word, freedom."[175] Totalitarian states, instead of fulfilling the duty of genuine authority to promote the autonomy of minor social unities, exterminates them, whether they be churches, universities, or chess clubs, and this extermination eventually undermines the efficiency of the whole.

In contrast, for Simon the best administration distributes responsibilities in such a way that it retains for itself the management of only those "over-all issues which do not admit of distribution."[176] The basic principle of growth of the Commonwealth coincides with democratic teaching on the decentralization of government, according to which the smaller, subsidiary community increases its jurisdiction over its own affairs, leaving to the federal sphere only those matters that properly belong to its jurisdiction: "No affair that can be managed by the local power should be taken care of by the power that is not the local power."[177] Since the progress of autonomy as part of natural law goes hand in hand with increased virtue and the genuine emancipation of mankind, Muñoz thought that those who insisted on opposing the principle of autonomy with regard to Puerto Rico were guilty of committing an unethical and anti-democratic deed:

> I do not doubt that there must be certain minds consciously or subconsciously *opposed to the democratic principle*, and that these minds really prefer that the people of Puerto Rico have less control over its destiny within the association, rather than more control over it within the association. Such a stand is neither responsible nor worthy of respect.[178]

Muñoz stressed that the development of Commonwealth should be undertaken without negatively affecting the other states of the union nor the United States in general. Whatever the details of the Commonwealth's development, the important principle is that development be mutually beneficial and bilateral, that is, subject to approval by both the Puerto Rican people and Congress. The standards to be used in the process of developing the Commonwealth are "the spiritual satisfaction of the people of Puerto Rico and the greatest prestige of the policies of the United States."[179]

Muñoz emphasized that progress in the autonomy of Puerto Rico, far from implying dissociation from the United States, meant a deeper and stronger union. He argued that the clearer the liberty of Puerto Rico, the closer the association would be, and that to the extent that this liberty seems reduced, the sense of the association would be weakened.[180] The association is between equal *personal* wholes, therefore, for ethical, political, pragmatic and aesthetic reasons, the comprehensive whole should not overwhelm the subsidiary whole. Muñoz believed that the more the political, cultural and economic autonomy of Puerto Rico grows, the better it would serve and contribute to the union, and the more willing and freely, since "loyalty to a political citizenship is more sincere and deeper if a culturally whole man can subscribe to it."[181]

Muñoz recognized other lines of growth for the Commonwealth of Puerto Rico. He believed, for example, that Puerto Rico should participate more intensely in international activities and organizations, so as "to serve the principle of inter-American solidarity better."[182] Since the remedial aspects of a healthy relationship diminish with time, Muñoz also included, among the lines of growth of the Commonwealth, that ways of contributing to the United States' Treasury, compatible with the status of association by compact, be devised for the time when Puerto Rico could pay taxes. Muñoz insisted from the beginning of the

Puerto Rico-United States relationship that tax exemption was
not to be taken as a principle by the people of Puerto Rico. He
observed that the Puerto Ricans are a proud people who do not
want anything for nothing. That Puerto Rico is not looking for
a "free ride" is proven, according to Muñoz, by the countless
Puerto Rican soldiers who have participated (a great many as
volunteers) and distinguished themselves in the wars of the American union.[183] Puerto Rico, said Muñoz, wants to contribute its
share. But the fact is that, in Muñoz's time, Puerto Rico simply
could not pay taxes because it did not have the money. Congress
itself recognized that it would have been absurd to exact taxes
from Puerto Rico at that time. Muñoz's position on this issue
was as follows:

> Puerto Rico ought to pay its share into the Fed-
> eral treasury as soon as it is in an economic posi-
> tion to do so in the same way that it is now con-
> tributing morally to the good democratic reputa-
> tion of the union. It would, however, be un-Chris-
> tian, uneconomic, un-American and extremely
> foolish for the Federal Treasury to exact such a con-
> tribution if that were to mean aggravating instead
> of diminishing poverty, surrendering health to dis-
> ease, closing instead of opening schools, lowering
> instead of improving standards of living, increas-
> ing instead of decreasing unemployment, and be-
> traying the wing of hope to the claw of despera-
> tion.[184]

NOTES

154. Luis Muñoz Marín, Speech delivered at Harvard University in Cambridge on 16 June 1955.

155. Muñoz Marín, Inaugural address delivered in San Juan on 2 January 1953.

156. Simon, *Philosophy of Democratic Government*, 7-19, 29-30.

157. Muñoz Marín, Speech delivered in Barranquitas on 17 July 1963; Speech delivered at the Rotary Club of San Juan on 19 June 1956; Message addressed to the people of Puerto Rico on the plebiscite on 19 August 1962.

158. See Chapter 1.

159. Simon, *Philosophy of Democratic Government*, 129; *Nature and Functions*, 46-47. Emphasis added.

160. Jacques Maritain, *Man and the State* (Chicago: The University of Chicago Press, 1951), 67.

161. Luis Muñoz Marín, "El status político de Puerto Rico," Speech delivered on 12 November 1954.

162. Muñoz Marín, Address delivered at the University of Kansas City on 23 April 1955.

163 See Chapter 1.

164. Simon, *Philosophy of Democratic Government*, 140.

165. Simon, *Freedom and Community*, 54.

166. Simon, "Common Good and Common Action, *The Review of Politics* 22 (1960): 233.

167. Ibid.

168. Ibid.

169. Yves R. Simon, *A General Theory of Authority*, with an introduction by Vukan Kuic (Notre Dame: University of Notre Dame Press, 1980), 15.

170. Ibid.

171. Simon, "Common Good and Common Action," 233.

172. Simon, *Philosophy of Democratic Government*, 129.

173. Pope Leo XIII, "Rerum Novarum," in *The Church Speaks to the Modern World. The Social Teachings of Leo XIII*, ed. Etienne Gilson (Garden City: Doubleday & Company, 1954), 235.

174. Simon, *Philosophy of Democratic Government*, 130.

175. Václav Havel, "The Post-Communist Nightmare," *The New York Review of Books*, 27 May 1993, 8.

176. Simon, *Philosophy of Democratic Government*, 131.

177. Muñoz Marín, Speech delivered at the Rotary Club of

San Juan on 19 June 1956. My translation.

178. Muñoz Marín, "The Political Status of Puerto Rico," Speech delivered on 12 November 1954. Emphasis added. See also Speech delivered at the Rotary Club of San Juan on 19 June 1956.

179. Muñoz Marín, Address delivered at the University of Kansas City on 23 April 1955.

180. Muñoz Marín, "La personalidad puertorriqueña en el Estado Libre Asociado."

181. Muñoz Marín, Inaugural address delivered in San Juan on 2 January 1953.

182. English translation of local House of Representatives concurrent resolution No. 21, *Para fijar la posición de la Asamblea Legislativa de Puerto Rico ante la Declaración Eisenhower sobre Puerto Rico*, 18 January 1954.

183. Muñoz Marín, "Puerto Rico Does Not Want to Be a State," 40.

184. Congress, Senate, Committee on Interior and Insular Affairs, *Statement before the Senate Committee on Interior and Insular Affairs*, 9 June 1959.

14410-RIVE

CONCLUSION

Puerto Rico had to create a new form of political freedom, because traditional formulas were not appropriate to it. In that enterprise it was Muñoz Marín who, like Hegel's "philosopher," interpreted the times and paved the way for a unique development of freedom. This new model of liberty which Puerto Rico exemplifies is not synonymous with independence, because it is not mere indeterminateness or optionality but is oriented towards the good, and the good for Puerto Rico involves an economic ideal not attainable—at least not in Muñoz's day—under the conditions of independence. Furthermore, the freedom brought forth by Puerto Rico surmounts the narrowness of nationalism, evincing the truth that real freedom is greater the more mastery one has over the means to achieve one's ends, a mastery that is enhanced in union and in that kind of participation within a wider whole and common good that is based on friendship and spiritual communion.

Nor does the freedom evidenced by Puerto Rico assume the form of a state of the American union, because, in the particular case of Puerto Rico, statehood would have meant the economic, political, and cultural absorption of the part by the whole, hence a violation of the principle of autonomy so well described by Simon. Besides loss of efficiency and impoverishment, both in the part and the whole (including the United States, the Caribbean and the rest of the world), the uniqueness of Puerto Rico would have been impaired, with the consequent destruction of life—both of the part and the whole—and the dissolution, the sterile homogenization, of enduring values such as language and culture. Since the principle of autonomy is not a mere policy but part of natural law, the passage from a status of more autonomy to one of less autonomy would not simply have been undemocratic, but a political injustice.

On the other hand, Puerto Rico, as a Commonwealth, serves and maximizes autonomy, which is the kind of freedom—oriented towards both the particular and the universal good—needed by the world at a time when the economic and ecological interdependence of all nations is recognized. Of course, whether a particular status, such as that of the Commonwealth, amounts to more net autonomy or integral liberty than another is a practical, prudential question. It cannot be decided a priori by a deduction from natural law. But if natural law includes the principle of autonomy, one can certainly foresee what the implications are of neglecting such a principle, acknowledging that, in general, a political status that maximizes autonomy rests not only on the soundest rational principles but on the highest democratic principles.

Two powerful forces have always worked to obstruct the growth of Commonwealth. First, the internal division caused by the Puerto Rican annexationist movement with the unnatural setback in autonomy and democracy it implies. This division not only prevents us from focusing on urgent local problems, but threatens to destroy us at last. The other force obstructing Commonwealth's progress has been the negligence with which the United States has dealt with the issue of the Puerto Rican political status. To mention but recent examples, Congress' decision (with the support of the local assimilationist government) to repeal Section 936 of the Federal Internal Revenue Code—Section on which Commonwealth bases the tax exemption strategies that propel its economy—has caused increasing unemployment and uncertainty in Puerto Rico, undermining the stability of Commonwealth. Another Congressional bill, the Young Bill, does not even recognize the legitimacy of Commonwealth or its right to, for example, receive the rum tariffs. This bill, backed by the local pro-statehood government, has already been approved by some subcommittees of the Federal House of Representatives.

All this takes place at a time ideal for doing just the opposite, namely, when the collapse of totalitarianism in Europe furnishes a foil against which American democracy can shine more conspicuously in the "showcase" of Commonwealth. Today it can be shown to the world, for example, that whereas totalitarian states overwhelm the economic, political and cultural autonomy of its citizens and of smaller institutions and communities, American democracy enhances the freedom of Commonwealth, and that whereas totalitarianism deprives peoples of their initiative, American democracy promotes the autonomy and self-sufficiency of Commonwealth.

Insofar as democracy deepens in the Commonwealth relationship, not only does the part (Puerto Rico) grow in freedom, but also the whole (the United States) is enhanced. Inversely, to the extent that federal laws apply in Puerto Rico without the *specific* consent of Puerto Ricans, laws that are unnecessary or even harmful for Puerto Rico and not essential to the association or to the national interest of the United States, the democratic principle is violated. Congress must live up to the compact of 1952 and the word of American presidents and leaders before the United Nations, and move, at last, not toward reducing but toward enhancing the freedom of the Commonwealth and the prestige of the United States. If the United States fails to perfect democracy in Puerto Rico, what can be expected by the rest of the world?

BIBLIOGRAPHY

Aquinas, St. Thomas. *Suma contra los gentiles.* Translated by Carlos Ignacio González, S.J. Mexico: Editorial Porrúa, 1991.

_____. *Summa Theologiae.* Translated by Fathers of the English Dominican Province. Westminster: Christian Classics, 1981.

Aristotle. *The Basic Works of Aristotle.* Edited by Richard McKeon. New York: Random House, 1971.

Benítez Rexach, Jesús. *Vida y obra de Luis Muñoz Marín.* Río Piedras: Editorial Edil, 1989.

Bernier, R. Elfrén. *Luis Muñoz Marín: líder y maestro.* Coamo: Anecdotario Mumarino I, 1988.

Bhana, Surenda. *The United States and the Development of the Puerto Rican Status Question, 1936-1968.* Lawrence: University Press of Kansas, 1975.

Bird Piñero, Enrique. *Don Luis Muñoz Marín: el poder de la excelencia.* Río Piedras: Fundación Luis Muñoz Marín, 1991.

Bothwell González, Reece B. *Puerto Rico: cien años de lucha política.* Río Piedras: Editorial Universitaria, 1979.

Cordua, Carla. *El mundo ético: ensayos sobre la esfera del hombre en la filosofía de Hegel.* Barcelona: Editorial Anthropos, 1989.

Davey, William George. "Luis Muñoz Marín: A Rhetorical Analysis of Political and Economic Modernization in Puerto Rico." Ph.D. diss., Indiana University, 1974.

Derisi, Octavio N. *Filosofía de la cultura y de los valores.* Buenos Aires: Emecé Editores, 1963.

Fernández Méndez, Eugenio, ed. *Unidad y esencia del "ethos" puertorriqueño.* Río Piedras: Universidad de Puerto Rico, 1954.

Fernós Isern, Antonio. *Estado Libre Asociado de Puerto Rico: antecedentes, creación y desarrollo hasta la época presente.* Río Piedras: Editorial Universitaria, 1974.

Gilson, Etienne. *The Christian Philosophy of St. Thomas Aquinas.* Translated by L.K. Shook, C.S.B. New York: Random House, 1956.

_____. *The Church Speaks to the Modern World. The Social Teachings of Leo XIII.* Garden City: Doubleday & Co., 1954.

Hernández Colón, Rafael. *La nueva tesis.* San Juan: Rafael Hernández Colón, 1979.

_____. *Retos y luchas.* San Juan: Rafael Hernández Colón, 1991.

Hunter, Robert John. "The Historical Evolution of the Relationship Between the United States and Puerto Rico (1898-1963)." Ph.D. diss., Pittsburg University, 1963.

Jameson, Howard Owen. "A Rhetorical Study of Luis Muñoz Marín and the Puerto Rican Political Status Controversy." Ph.D. diss., Temple University, 1971.

John of St. Thomas. *Cursus philosophicus thomisticus, secundum exactam, veram, genuinam Aristotelis et Doctoris Angelici mentem.* Edited by P. Beato Reiser O.S.B. Rome: Marietti, 1929.

Labarthe, Pedro Juan. *¿Quién es el gobernador de Puerto Rico?* San José, Costa Rica: Repertorio Americano, 1949.

Lidin, Harold. *History of the Puerto Rican Independence Movement.* 3 vols. Hato Rey: Master Typesetting de Puerto Rico, 1981.

Mahoney, Marianne. "Prudence as the Cornerstone of the Contemporary Thomistic Philosophy of Freedom." In *Freedom in the Modern World: Jacques Maritain, Yves R. Simon, Mortimer J. Adler,* ed. Michael D. Torre, 117-29. Notre Dame: University of Notre Dame Press, 1989.

Maritain, Jacques. *Cristianismo y democracia.* Translated by Héctor F. Miri. Buenos Aires: Editorial Dedalo, 1961.

_____. *Du régime temporel et de la liberté.* Paris: Desclée de Brouwer et Cie., 1933.

_____. *Man and the State.* Chicago: The University of Chicago Press, 1951.

_____. *The Person and the Common Good.* Translated by John J. Fitzgerald. London: Geoffrey Bles, 1948.

_____. *The Rights of Man and Natural Law.* Translated by Doris C. Anson. New York: Charles Scribner's Sons, 1951.

_____. *Siete lecciones sobre el ser y los primeros principios de la razón especulativa.* Translated by Alfredo E. Frossard. Buenos Aires: Desclée, de Brouwer, 1944.

Mathews, Thomas G. *Luis Muñoz Marín: A Concise Biography*. New York: American R.D.M. Corp., 1967.

Morales Carrión, Arturo. *Puerto Rico and the United States: The Quest for A New Encounter*. San Juan: Editorial Académica, 1990.

_____, ed. *Puerto Rico: A Political and Cultural History*. New York: W.W. Norton, 1983.

Muñoz Marín, Luis. Address delivered at Bate College in Maine on 9 June 1957. *Archivo Luis Muñoz Marín, Fundación Luis Muñoz Marín*, Río Piedras, Puerto Rico.

_____. Address delivered on 4 July 1964. *Archivo Luis Muñoz Marín*.

_____. Address delivered at the University of Kansas City on 23 April 1955. *Archivo Luis Muñoz Marín*.

_____. "An America to Serve the World." Speech delivered on 7 April 1956. *Archivo Luis Muñoz Marín*.

_____. "Breakthrough from Nationalism: A Small Island Looks at Big Trouble." The Godkin Lectures given at Harvard University, Cambridge on 28-30 April 1959. *Archivo Luis Muñoz Marín*.

_____. "Cultura y democracia." Speech delivered at the *Foro del Ateneo Puertorriqueño* in San Juan on 1940. *Archivo Luis Muñoz Marín*.

_____. "The Deep Significance of United States Citizenship." English translation of the address delivered on the occasion of the fourth anniversary of the Commonwealth of Puerto Rico on 25 July 1956. *Archivo Luis Muñoz Marín*.

_____. "Del tiempo de Muñoz Rivera a nuestro tiempo." Speech delivered on 17 July 1956. *Archivo Luis Muñoz Marín.*

_____. "Development Through Democracy." *The Annals of the American Academy of Political and Social Science* 285 (1953): 1-8.

_____. *Discursos oficiales: pensamiento político, económico, social y cultural (1949-1952).* With an Introduction by Gustavo Agrait. Los gobernadores electos de Puerto Rico. Río Piedras: Corporación de Servicios Bibliotecarios, 1973.

_____. English translation of the address delivered on the occasion of the fifth anniversary of the Commonwealth of Puerto Rico on 25 July 1957. *Archivo Luis Muñoz Marín.*

_____. English translation of a message addressed to the people of Puerto Rico on the plebiscite on 19 August 1962. *Archivo Luis Muñoz Marín.*

_____. English translation of notes for a speech delivered at the Convention of the San Juan Popular Youth on 13 March 1960. *Archivo Luis Muñoz Marín.*

_____. "Facts Forum's State of the Nation." Transcript of radio program in which Muñoz is interviewed by Harwood Hull in San Juan on 9 March 1954. *Archivo Luis Muñoz Marín.*

_____. *Foreign Policy Review: Hearing held before the Committee on Foreign Relations.* Statement before Congress, Committee on Foreign Relations on 10 March 1958. *Archivo Luis Muñoz Marín.*

_____. Inaugural address delivered in San Juan on 2 January 1953. *Archivo Luis Muñoz Marín.*

_____. *La historia del Partido Popular Democrático.* San Juan: Editorial El Batey, 1984.

_____. *Memorias: autobiografía pública 1898-1940.* With an Introduction by Jaime Benítez. San Juan: Inter American University Press, 1982.

_____. *Memorias: autobiografía pública (1940-1952).* With an Introduction by Jaime Benítez. San Germán: Universidad Interamericana de Puerto Rico, 1992.

_____. *Mensajes al pueblo puertorriqueño.* With an Introduction by Antonio J. Colorado. San Juan: Inter American University Press, 1980.

_____. Notes for a speech delivered at the Rotary Club of San Juan on 28 July 1953. *Archivo Luis Muñoz Marín.*

_____. "La personalidad puertorriqueña en el Estado Libre Asociado." Speech addressed at the *Asamblea General de la Asociación de Maestros de Puerto Rico* on 29 December 1953. *Archivo Luis Muñoz Marín.*

_____. "The Political Status of Puerto Rico." English translation of a speech delivered on 12 November 1954. *Archivo Luis Muñoz Marín.*

_____. "Puerto Rico Does Not Want to Be a State." *The New York Times Magazine,* 16 August 1959, 19.

_____. "Puerto Rico's Role in International Cooperation." Address delivered at the Inaugural Session of the ICA Conference of Mission Directors and Program Staff of Latin American Area in San Juan on 27 January 1958. *Archivo Luis Muñoz Marín.*

_____. *Puerto Rico y los Estados Unidos: su futuro en común.* San Juan: Editorial del Departamento de Instrucción Pública, 1954.

_____. "Significación del Estado Libre Asociado de Puerto Rico en la Unión americana." Speech delivered at the Annual Assembly of the Chamber of Commerce of Puerto Rico in San Juan on 14 February 1958. *Archivo Luis Muñoz Marín.*

_____. Speech delivered at the *Asamblea General de la Asociación de Maestros* in San Juan on 28 December 1962. *Archivo Luis Muñoz Marín.*

_____. Speech delivered at the *Asamblea del Parque Sixto Escobar* in San Juan on 24 August 1952. *Archivo Luis Muñoz Marín.*

_____. Speech delivered at the *Asociación de Alcaldes* in San Juan on 1959. *Archivo Luis Muñoz Marín.*

_____. Speech delivered in Barranquitas, Puerto Rico on 17 July 1951. *Archivo Luis Muñoz Marín.*

_____. Speech delivered in Barranquitas on 17 July 1963. *Archivo Luis Muñoz Marín.*

_____. Speech delivered at the Congreso Interamericano de Municipalidades on 3 December 1954. *Archivo Luis Muñoz Marín.*

_____. Speech delivered at the Graduation Ceremony of the *Universidad Católica de Santa María* in Ponce, Puerto Rico on 22 May 1964. *Archivo Luis Muñoz Marín.*

_____. Speech delivered at Harvard University in Cambridge on 16 June 1955. *Archivo Luis Muñoz Marín.*

_____. Speech delivered at the Lions Club of San Juan on 22 July 1959. *Archivo Luis Muñoz Marín.*

_____. Speech delivered at the Lions Club of San Juan on 4 November 1959. *Archivo Luis Muñoz Marín.*

_____. Speech delivered in Maricao, Puerto Rico on 17 September 1952. *Archivo Luis Muñoz Marín.*

_____. Speech delivered at the National Press Club in Washington, D.C. on 18 June 1957. *Archivo Luis Muñoz Marín.*

_____. Speech delivered on the occasion of the first anniversary of the Commonwealth of Puerto Rico in San Juan on 25 July 1953. *Archivo Luis Muñoz Marín.*

_____. Speech delivered on the occasion of an homage paid to Muñoz at the Hotel San Juan in Isla Verde, Puerto Rico on 19 February 1961. *Archivo Luis Muñoz Marín.*

_____. Speech delivered on the occasion of receiving the Award of Liberty granted by the House of Liberty on 7 October 1956. *Archivo Luis Muñoz Marín.*

_____. Speech delivered at a Press Club Luncheon in Washington, D. C. on 6 May 1952. *Archivo Luis Muñoz Marín.*

_____. Speech delivered at the Rotary Club of San Juan on 19 June 1956. *Archivo Luis Muñoz Marín.*

_____. Speech delivered at the Rotary Club of Santurce, Puerto Rico on 12 November 1958. *Archivo Luis Muñoz Marín.*

_____. *Statement before the Senate Committee on Interior and Insular Affairs.* Statement before Congress, Committee on Interior and Insular Affairs, on 9 June 1959. *Archivo Luis Muñoz Marín.*

_____. "El status político de Puerto Rico." Speech delivered on 3 June 1959. *Archivo Luis Muñoz Marín.*

_____. "El status político de Puerto Rico." Speech delivered on 4 June 1959. *Archivo Luis Muñoz Marín.*

_____. "The Status of Puerto Rico." Speech delivered on 12 March 1959. *Archivo Luis Muñoz Marín.*

Nelson Tuck, Jay and Norma C. Vergara. "Hope Moves the People. Luis Muñoz Marín." In *Heroes of Puerto Rico.* New York: Fleet Press Corporation, 1969.

Ortiz Salichs, Ana M. and María Hernández Rodríguez, eds. *Luis Muñoz Marín: bibliografía mínima.* Ponce: Centro de Estudios Puertorriqueños, 1991.

Pagán, Bolívar. *Historia de los partidos políticos puertorriqueños (1898-1956).* San Juan: Librería Campos, 1959.

Plato. *The Collected Dialogues of Plato.* Edited by Edith Hamilton and Huntington Cairns. Princeton: Princeton University Press, 1978.

Ramírez Lavandero, Marcos, ed. *Documents of the Constitutional Relationship of Puerto Rico and the United States.* Washington, D.C.: Puerto Rico Federal Affairs Administration, n.d.

Ramos, Aarón Gamaliel. *Las ideas anexionistas en Puerto Rico bajo la dominación norteamericana*. Río Piedras: Ediciones Huracán, 1987.

Ramos de Santiago, Carmen, ed. *El desarrollo constitucional de Puerto Rico: documentos y casos*. Río Piedras: Editorial Universidad de Puerto Rico, 1973.

Rasmussen, Douglas B. and Douglas J. Den Uyl. *Liberty and Nature: An Aristotelian Defense of Liberal Order*. La Salle, Illinois: Open Court, 1991.

Rivera, José A. "Political Autonomy and the Good in the Thought of Yves R. Simon and Luis Muñoz Marín." Ph.D. diss., The Catholic University of America, 1993.

Robles de Cardona, Mariana. *Búsqueda y plasmación de nuestra personalidad*. San Juan: Editorial Club la Prensa, 1958.

_____. *El gobierno de Puerto Rico*. Río Piedras: Editorial Universitaria, 1970.

Rosario Natal, Carmelo. *La juventud de Luis Muñoz Marín: vida y pensamiento, 1898-1932*. San Juan: Master Typesetting de Puerto Rico, 1976.

_____. ed. *Luis Muñoz Marín: juicios sobre su significado histórico*. San Juan: 1990.

Rourke, Thomas R. and Clarke E. Cochran. "The Common Good and Economic Justice: Reflections on the Thought of Yves R. Simon." *The Review of Politics* 52 (1992): 231-52.

Sánchez Tarniella, Andrés. *Contradicciones en las distintas alternativas políticas*. Río Piedras: Ediciones Bayoán, 1979.

_____. *El dilema puertorriqueño: lenguaje de libertad o lenguaje de dominación, una tesis sobre la liberación de Puerto Rico.* San Juan: Ediciones Bayoán, 1973.

_____. *El plebiscito de los anexionistas: culminación de sus "cien años de soledad."* Río Piedras: Ediciones Bayoán, 1993.

_____. *La batalla de los adoquines: identidad vs. lumpenización.* Río Piedras: Ediciones Bayoán, 1981.

_____. *La economía de Puerto Rico.* Río Piedras, Puerto Rico: Ediciones Bayoán, 1973.

_____. "La política y la crisis". En *Sobre la identidad nacional.* Río Piedras: Ediciones Bayoán, 1981.

_____. *Los costos de la estadidad para Puerto Rico.* Río Piedras: Ediciones Bayoán, 1980.

_____. *Nuevo enfoque sobre el desarrollo político de Puerto Rico.* Río Piedras: Ediciones Bayoán, 1972.

_____. *Trayectoria de las actitudes políticas en Puerto Rico.* Río Piedras: Ediciones Bayoán, 1975.

Simon, Yves R. *A General Theory of Authority.* With an Introduction by Vukan Kuic. Notre Dame: University of Notre Dame Press, 1980.

_____. "Common Good and Common Action." *The Review of Politics* 22 (1960): 202-44.

_____. *The Community of the Free.* Translated by Willard R. Task. New York: Holt & Co., 1947.

_____. *The Definition of Moral Virtue.* Edited by Vukan Kuic. New York: Fordham University Press, 1986.

_____. "The Doctrinal Issue between the Church and Democracy." In *The Catholic Church and World Affairs,* ed. Waldemar Gurian and Matthew A. Fitzsimons, 87-114. Notre Dame: University of Notre Dame Press, 1954.

_____. "Economic Organization in a Democracy." *Proceedings of the American Catholic Philosophical Association* 20 (1945): 83-108.

_____. *Freedom and Community.* Edited by Charles P. O'Donnell. New York: Fordham University Press, 1968.

_____. *Freedom of Choice.* Edited by Peter Wolff. With a Foreword by Mortimer Adler. New York: Fordham University Press, 1969.

_____. "Law and Liberty." *The Review of Politics* 52 (1990): 107-18.

_____. "Liberty and Authority." *Proceedings of the American Catholic Philosophical Association* 16 (1940): 86-114.

_____. *The March to Liberation.* Translated by Victor M. Hamm. Milwaukee: The Tower Press, 1942.

_____. "Más allá de la crisis del liberalismo." In *Ensayos sobre el tomismo,* ed. Robert E. Brennan, trans. P. Efrén Villacorte, 345-373. Madrid: Ediciones Morata, 1962.

_____. *Nature and Functions of Authority.* The Aquinas Lecture. Milwaukee: Marquette University Press, 1940.

_____. *Philosophy of Democratic Government*. Chicago: The University of Chicago Press, 1951.

_____. *Practical Knowledge*. Edited by Robert J. Mulvaney. New York: Fordham University Press, 1991.

_____. "Thomism and Democracy." In *Science, Philosophy and Religion*. Second Symposium. Vol. 2. Edited by Louis Finkelstein and Lyman Bryson, 258-72. New York: The Conference on Science, Philosophy and Religion in their Relation to the Democratic Way of Life, Inc., 1942.

_____. *The Tradition of Natural Law: A Philosopher's Reflection*. Edited by Vukan Kuic. With a Foreword by John H. Hallowell. New York: Fordham University Press, 1965.

Sokolowski, Robert. *The God of Faith and Reason: Foundations of Christian Theology*. Notre Dame: University of Notre Dame Press, 1982.

Sorel, Georges. *Reflections on Violence*. Translated by T.E. Hulme. New York: B.W. Huebsch, 1914.

Tió, Salvador. *Desde el Tuétano*. San Juan: Editorial Cultural, 1992.

_____. *Lengua mayor: ensayos sobre el español de aquí y de allá*. Río Piedras: Editorial Plaza Mayor, 1991.

Torregrosa, Angel M. *Luis Muñoz Marín, 1898-1944; su vida y su patriótica obra*. San Juan: Editorial Esther, 1944.

Trías Monge, José. *Historia constitucional de Puerto Rico*. Río Piedras: Editorial Universidad de Puerto Rico, 1980.

Tugwell, R.G. *The Art of Politics, As Practiced by Three Great Americans: Franklin Delano Roosevelt, Luis Muñoz Marín and Fiorello H. La Guardia.* New York: Doubleday, 1958.

Van Doren, Charles. "The Idea of Freedom." 2 parts. In *The Great Ideas Today*, ed. Robert M. Hutchins and Mortimer J. Adler, 300-392, 232-300. Chicago: Encyclopedia Britannica, 1972 and 1973.

Velázquez Net, Ismaro. *Muñoz y Sánchez Vilella.* Río Piedras: Editorial Universitaria, 1974.